● Cultural China Series

Li Song

CHINESE BRONZE WARE

A Mirror of Culture

Translated by Zhu Jianting, Li Li & He Yunzhao

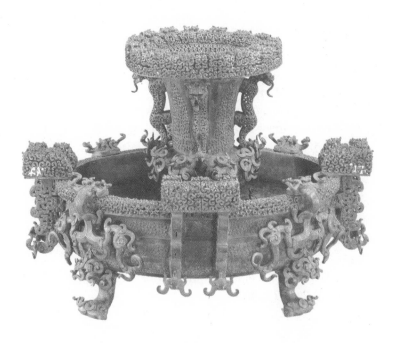

CHINA
INTERCONTINENTAL
PRESS

图书在版编目（CIP）数据

中国青铜器／李松著；朱建廷，李莉，何云朝译．—北京：五洲传播出版社，2009.1

ISBN 978-7-5085-1325-6

I.中... II.①李...②朱...③李...④何... III.青铜器（考古）－简介－中国 IV.K876.41-49

中国版本图书馆CIP数据核字（2008）第058024号

CHINESE BRONZE WARE

A Mirror of Culture

Author: Li Song

Translator: Zhu Jianting, Li Li & He Yunzhao

Executive Editor: Su Qian

Art Director: Tian Lin

Publisher: China Intercontinental Press (6 Beixiaomachang, Lianhuachi Donglu, Haidian District, Beijing 100038, China)

Tel: 86-10-58891281

Website: www.cicc.org.cn

Printer: C&C Joint Printing Co., (Beijing) Ltd.

Format: 720×965mm   1/16

Signatures: 10

Words: 95,000

Print Run: 1-5000

Edition: Jan. 2009, 1st edition, 1st print run

Price: RMB 92.00 (*yuan*)

Contents

Preface

Copper is the earliest known metal that was used by humankind. As early as the late the Neolithic Age, ancient people discovered natural copper which has a golden color and luster and high ductility. They cherished the metal and made small adornments or knives with it. Unfortunately, copper is not hard enough to be applied extensively. Later on, people mastered the technology to smelt copper from ore and add appropriate stannum or plumbum into it to increase its hardness and decrease its melting point. Thus, the processed metal, easier to be founded and resistant to abrasiveness, can be used in manufacturing production instruments, household utensils and weaponry. It is now what we call bronze.

The debut of bronze ware marks an important leap in the history of civilization. Bronze ware changed people's living and working conditions and greatly improved the entire society's productivity. As a result, industry and all aspects of society experienced profound transformations, eventually establishing classes and countries. From that moment, human society ended the Stone Age and entered into the new Bronze Age.

Numerous existing bronze ware in China are mainly from archeological excavation. Some were discovered in ancient times and kept until today, but many more were unearthed in modern archeological digs.

Different from the bronze culture of other countries and regions, ancient China attached grand religious and political significance to bronze ware. Through the monopoly of raw bronze materials and the smelting and foundry technology, the ruling slaveholders, following their plans, founded bronze ware in various shapes representing their political rights, military power and wealth or even the regime of the country.

The discovery and application of bronze also opened up a new area for art creation. In the Shang (c. 1600–c. 1046 BC) and Western Zhou (c. 1046–c. 771 BC) dynasties, the variety of shapes, the enormous volumes, the mystery and complexity of patterns, the abundance of inscriptions of various bronze ware had a spiritual connotation that all art work created with different materials previously used could not reach. Therefore, bronze art had ascended the second stage of art since color pottery art in primitive society in ancient China.

Bronze Age

The term of Bronze Age can be traced back to the first half of the 19th century. In 1918, Danish scholar C. J. Thomsen (1788–1865), who curated an antique exhibition at the National Museum of Denmark, defined a time sequence of three comparatively independent ages: Stone Age, Bronze Age (including brass), and Iron Age, gradually generally recognized in history circles from then on.

Archeological discovery proves all ancient cultures experienced the Bronze Age. In Egypt, bronze ware debuted in the Middle Kingdom period (2133–1786 BC) and reached its peak in the New Kingdom period (1567–1085 BC). In Mesopotamia, bronze ware appeared in the First Dynasty of Ur (c. 2700–2371 BC) and prevailed in the Third Dynasty of Ur (c. 2133–2006 BC). The Bronze Age of the Indus Valley occurred in the period of Harappan Culture (c. 2350–1750 BC).

China's Bronze Age experienced a 2,000-year-long period starting from the Xia (c. 2070–1600 BC), Shang (1600–1046 BC) to Zhou (1046–256 BC, including Western and Eastern Zhou) dynasties, is later than ancient Egypt and Mesopotamia. However, China's bronze ware holds a unique position in civilization's history compared to the rest of the world, thanks to its complicated varieties, distinct forms and sophisticated metallurgical technologies.

According to ancient literature, records on the excavation and appreciation of bronze ware of the said three dynasties appear in the Western Han Dynasty (206 BC–AD 25). With the boom of sphragistics in the Song Dynasty (960–1279), drawings and catalogues of ancient bronze ware as well as research on inscriptions, patterns, forms, structures, names and production years, the Qing Dynasty (1616–1911) witnessed the heyday of sphragistics and textual criticism of bronze ware. But, research on inscriptions, forms and structures were pervasive through the mutual verification between the inscribed wording and historic classics in this period. However, the study of the extensive amount of bronze ware from the aspect of art history began from research on stage division and style evolution, of which the foundation was mainly laid in the 1930s. Modern science and archeology study explains more and more, the social politics, economy and cultural background of the origin and development of ancient bronze ware, providing confirmation with literature and reliable evidence of the production motivation and more profound understanding of humanistic connotations and art achievements.

Bronze Ware in the Xia Dynasty

Ancient Chinese believe that the origin of bronze ware is mysterious and sacred. Many vivid myths and legends on the origin of bronze are spread over past dynasties. Up to now, the earliest bronze ware, cast in 3000 BC or so that was discovered in China, were bronze knives and some bronze ware relics unearthed in Dongxiang, Gansu in 1975.

Ancient Chinese deemed bronze cooking vessels for sacrifices were most noble. Ancient literature indicates that the earliest casting of bronze *Ding* (caldron with tripod legs) started at 2100 BC, the beginning of the Xia Dynasty, the first national regime in Chinese history. It is said that Xia's founder Yu and his son Qi issued decrees to cast nine large bronze *Ding*. They were later passed down in the Xia, Shang and Zhou dynasties.

The Xia Dynasty's 470-year-long reign was a burgeoning

Xia. *Jue*
20.7cm high. Unearthed in Erlitou, Yanshi, Henan in 1984. Kept in the Archaeology Research Institute of the Chinese Academy of Social Sciences.

period in Chinese bronze art. However, a previous lengthy period of more than 20 centuries had passed since the discovery and use of natural copper until bronze smelting and bronze ware production.

Archeological discoveries from the Xia Dynasty chiefly include the late period of Henan's Longshan Culture (2700–2100 BC) and Yanshi Erlitou Culture (1800–1600 BC), situated in today's middle and western Henan and southern Shanxi provinces.

Many Xia Dynasty bronze ware were excavated from these sites, including production tools like knives, chisels, awls and barbs, weapons such as dagger-axes, axes, arrowheads, vessels of *Jue* (an ancient wine vessel with three legs and a loop handle), *Gu* (a beaker), *He* (ancient utensil) and other containers. However, traditional *Ding* were not unearthed there.

In the Xia Dynasty, bronze ware processing applied similar pottery shapes as the model. Some bronze *Jue* and *He* unearthed at the Erlitou site are similar with the pottery counterparts in their shapes. However, some bronze ware moved away from pottery forms and structures, resulting in forging its own independent designs.

The production of quite sophisticated bronze *Jue* and other vessels indicates the Xia made great progress in bronze casting technology. A model with intended shapes were first fabricated with clay for bronze ware casting. A single model was enough for casting simple items like knives and arrowheads. Two models were required for more complicated ware. For vessels like *Jue* and *Ding*, several models and inner models were necessary and some accessory components had to be welded together.

The Xia Dynasty's bronze vessels seldom have simple patterns. On the contrary, the unearthed bronze plates of the same period, boasting elaborated designs, production

Erlitou Relics

Erlitou Relics, located at Erlitou Village, Yanshi, Henan province, was discovered in 1959. For a long time, there were two different opinions about Erlitou Culture in the academic circle: some experts believed Phase I to Phase IV of Erlitou Relics belonged to the cultural relics of Xia Dynasty (2100 –1600BC) and the place where the relics were discovered was the capital of Xia. Others believed Phase I and II were cultural relics of the Xia Dynasty, but Phase III and Phase IV were relics of the Shang Dynasty (1600–1100BC) and the place was the capital of Shang. With the completeion of the Xia and Shang periodization program, most scholars accepted the opinion that the major part of Erlitou Culture was relics of the Xia Dynasty and Erlitou was the capital of the middle and late Xia Dynasty.

and complicated turquoise mosaics, considered the most exquisite artwork created by the Xia's bronze craftsmen.

Xia. Bronze Plate Decoration embedded with kalliate 16.5cm long. Unearthed in Erlitou, Yanshi, Henan in 1984. Kept in the Archaeology Research Institute of the Chinese Academy of Social Sciences. It is the earliest discovery of a Taotie image. Several pieces of similar works were found with the image varying slightly.

The bronze plates, unearthed from tombs of noble families and found at the owners' waists, are square, round in edges and corners, and slightly narrower in the middle. The plate, having two holes on each side, is presumed to be an ornament that was sewn on hemp clothes or used as an amulet to protect against evils or devils. Nearly a hundred different and fine-ground turquoise pieces were orderly arranged to form an eye-popped *Taotie* (a mythical ferocious animal) through rigid design and calculation. This is the early form of the *Taotie* theme, which became the dominant decoration on bronze ware in the following Shang and Zhou dynasties.

Jewelry-inlaid bronze ware has the beautiful name of "gold inlaid with jade." The combination of jewelry and bronze enriched the form and ornamentation of bronze ware. This technology was constantly developed from then onwards and was prevalent in the later Spring and Autumn (770–476 BC) and Warring States (475–221 BC) periods, contributing to the brilliant and gorgeous appearances of the bronze ware in those days.

The Xia Dynasty's bronze plates demonstrate China's bronze

ware casting entered a mature period very early to the later generations. The craftsmen not only focused on the practical use of these items, but also presented their definite aesthetic intentions.

Bronze Ware in the Shang Dynasty

The Shang Dynasty, the second slavery dynasty in China's history, was established in 1600 BC under the leadership of eastern tribes chief Tang after ending the Xia Dynasty and lasted about 600 years. After frequent relocations of the capital in the early period, Emperor Pangeng moved it to Yin (today's Anyang, Henan) in 1300 BC and settled there for 273 years. Emperor Wuding succeeded the throne in 1250 BC, marking the heyday of the Shang Dynasty. Historians regard the period before Emperor Wuding's reign as the early Shang Dynasty and the period during and after Emperor Wuding as the late Shang Dynasty.

Unearthed bronze ware in Zhengzhou, Henan, the capital of the early Shang Dynasty, indicates one-meter-high and 82kg large squares that were made at that time. The varieties of bronze ware are generally complete pieces.

The late Shang Dynasty witnessed the first culmination of China's bronze art. Thousands of bronze ware excavated from the Yin Ruins (*Yinxu*) were found to be complete in varieties, diversified shapes, beautiful patterns and sophisticated casting, showcasing the high maturity of the Shang Dynasty's bronze ware art. In addition, a lot of bronze ware cast in the late Shang Dynasty was also unearthed in Hebei, Shaanxi, Shanxi, Shandong, An'hui and Liaoning provinces. South of the Yangtze River Valley, the bronze culture close to the Shang Culture with intense local color were also discovered at Sanxingdui site, Guanghan, Sichuan, Dayangzhou Site, Xingan, Jiangxi and

Shang. *Ding*
95cm high. Unearthed in
Dayangzhou, Xingan, Jiangxi in
1989. Kept in Jiangxi Museum.

some other sites in Hunan.

During the world's early civilized period, bronze was mostly used in casting tools of production and living. However, China's bronze ware had unique features. After the development of a class society, utensils, wine and water vessels and other daily ware were exclusively owned by slave owners and nobles, resulting in the functions evolving into ritual and divine ware for sacrifices, banquets, funerals and so forth.

As a dynasty worshipping immortals and spirits, wealth and violence, the nobles and rulers of Shang always prayed for a better future, for the enlightenment and blessing of deities and ancestors. In the frequent and

Anyang Yin Ruins
Yin Ruins is located on both banks of Huanhe River, northwest suburb of Anyang, Henan province. It was developed into a grand capital of about 30 sq km in total with 273 years of development from Emperor Pangeng who moved the capital to Yin to Shang's last Emperor Xin. In the 1890s, oracle bone inscriptions were found in Yin Ruins. Since 1928, all-round and continuous archeological efforts have been made in Yin Ruins. Palace, workshop and tombs were found and a great deal of oracle bones, bronze ware and jade ware were unearthed.

Shang. *Chixiao You*
19.7cm high in total. Unearthed from Erlangpo, Shilou county, Shanxi Province in 1957. Kept in Shanxi Museum.

grand sacrifices, bronze ware played a crucial role: various bronze wine vessels, such as different-sized *Jue, Zun* and *You* filled with wine were displayed on the altar; cooked meals were served in bronze *Ding* and put into small bronze meal vessels like small *Ding* and *Gui* to entertain deities and ancestors. Emperors, grand nobles and other similarly privileged classes were the only ones to perform auguries and sacrifices.

The Shang Dynasty's people believed the soul remains upon death. The deceased emperors and

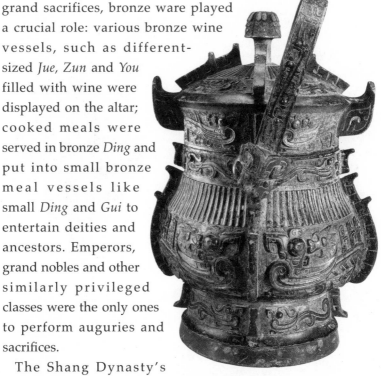

Shang . *Fuding You*
35.5cm high. Kept in Shanghai Museum.

nobles were buried together with a great number of persons and livestock as well as many bronze and jade ware. A surprising discovery of a well-preserved large tomb of a nobleman at the Yin ruins in Anyang in 1976 offers a complete display of the deluxe underground palace of the nobles from the Shang Dynasty. The occupant of the tomb was a spouse of Emperor Wuding. Among the unearthed 1,928 pieces of funerary objects from the tomb, 468 pieces were bronze ware including 210 were ritual bronze ware. Extant bronze ware made in the Shang Dynasty are mostly found in similar tombs and tombs of nobles.

The then social characteristic of "ghosts superior than

rituals" added a rigid, authoritarian and mysterious personality to bronze ware of the Shang Dynasty. Bronze ware's enormous volume, unsophisticated shape and pervasive mysterious pattern emanated a silent psychological deterrence. In terms of aesthetics, bronze ware in the Shang Dynasty had a kind of "ferocious beauty." A great number of well-known heavy bronze ware of the period, such as *Simuwu Ding, Oufang Yi, Dragon and Tiger Zun, Four-goat Square Zun*, reflect the spirit and culture of that period.

Shang. Bronze Double-face Figure
52cm high. Unearthed from Dayangzhou, Xingan county, Jiangxi Province in 1989. The figure is hollow, and has two identical faces.

Bronze Ware in the Western Zhou Dynasty

The Zhou clan, growing up in the northwestern regions, established the Zhou Dynasty after defeating the Shang Dynasty under Emperor Wuwang in 1046 BC. Several nobles, who associated with the then ethic group Quan Rong, captured the capital Haojing and killed Emperor Youwang of the Zhou Dynasty in 771 BC. The nearly 300-year-long period starting from Emperor Wuwang to Emperor Youwang is called the Western Zhou Dynasty in Chinese history.

The bronze art achievements of the late Shang directly followed into the Western Zhou Dynasty. Consistent with the Shang

Dynasty, bronze ware was still deemed as symbols of regime and theocracy. With the change of political system and auxiliary religious rites, the spiritual connotation of the Western Zhou's bronze culture experienced crucial and essential changes.

At the beginning of the Western Zhou Dynasty, one of the important political measures adopted was the practice of fiefdoms. The basis for fiefdoms is the kin-tied patriarchal clan system with the lineal eldest son succession as the core concept. The patriarchal clan system defines the hierarchy and succession relationship, the rights and duties of the then noble class, consisting of the emperor, nobles, ministers and scholar-officials.

Rites and music systems closely echoed the patriarchal clan system. The aim of promoting rites and music was to "harmonize through music and order through rites" amongst the nobles.

Ritual and musical bronze ware of the Western Zhou Dynasty, as the carriers of the then patriarchal clan system and the musical and ritual system, were rigidly restricted to the user's position and rank in varieties, size and quantity. For instance, according

Western Zhou. *Tianwang Gui*
24.2cm high, spout diameter 21cm, standing border 18.5cm long. It is said Tianwang Gui was unearthed from Qishan, Shaanxi during the reign of Emperor Daoguang (1782–1850), Qing Dynasty (1644–1911). Kept in the National Museum of China.
It has an inscription of 77 Chinese characters, recording the event of the Emperor Wuwang of the Zhou Dynasty defeating the Emperor of Shang.

Western Zhou. Chunhua Big *Ding*
122cm high, spout diameter 83cm, and weighs 226kg. Unearthed from Chunhua county, Shaanxi in 1979. Kept in Chunhua County Museum.
The largest bronze *Ding* of the Western Zhou Dynasty.

to ancient records, in the Western Zhou's ritual ceremonies, the *Ding*, which had a core position of various bronze ware, the Emperor could use nine, the nobles seven, the scholar officials five and the scholar three.

Since the bronze ritual ware had the function of identifying hierarchy, those used by emperors and nobles became the symbols of the country and the regime. As a result, a victorious nation not only looted the wealth of the defeated nation and captured its fiefdoms but also took away the bronze ritual ware out of the losing country's ancestral temple. It was the so-called "destroying its ancestral temple and taking away its vital bronze ware" in the ancient books.

Different from the Shang Dynasty's fashion of "leading the people to offer sacrifices to deities and paying higher respect to ghosts than rituals," the Zhou Dynasty's people paid higher respects to rites and "stayed at a respectful distance from deities." Under such social influence, the bronze ware cast in the Zhou Dynasty gradually evolved to become more common and more practical, presenting a solemn art style instead of the eerie and

Western Zhou. *Zhe Gong*
28.7cm high, 38cm long, and weighs 6.7kg. Discovered in Fufeng county, Shaanxi in 1976. Kept in Zhouyuan Cultural Relics Administration.
The cap and vessel share the same inscription of four lines totaling 40 Chinese characters, recording the noble Zhe was awarded by the Emperor of the Zhou Dynasty because of his merits and made the vessel for his father Yi.

Western Zhou. Bronze Square Kettle
49cm high. Excavated from the Guoguo tomb,
Sanmenxia, Henan Province in 1990. Kept in Henan
Cultural Relics Research Institute.

mysterious color in the previous dynasty.

Extant bronze ware of the Western Dynasty was mainly unearthed in Zhouyuan prefecture (between Qishan and Fufeng counties, Shaanxi Province), cradle of the Zhou clan, and Fengjing and Haojing (on both sides of Feng River in Chang'an County, Shaanxi Province), which were capitals of the dynasty. Most of them were ware used by nobles and ministers. A great number of those, possibly buried by nobles on their hurried escape during social turmoil, were excavated from cellars. Many bronze ware were awarded by the emperor, exchanged among kingdoms or cast by themselves were unearthed in the regions of kingdoms.

The evolution of the Western Zhou Dynasty's bronze art experiences rose and fell. Some key representative work mostly appeared in the early and late period. The works in the early Zhou Dynasty were quite similar to the ware in the late Shang Dynasty in the aspect of varieties, shapes, patterns and accessories. Only individual ware and patterns have differences. In addition, bronze ware always had long inscriptions on the surface in this period, which is considered an outstanding feature of the bronze ware from the Western Zhou Dynasty.

During the middle period from Emperor Muwang (976–922 BC) to Emperor Yiwang (885–877 BC), there were great changes in the types, shapes and patterns. The popular wine vessels gradually disappeared and other items changed. Utensils became dominant, and chimes were used as instruments. The curled, ripple and ribbon pattern and other abstract designs replaced the Shang Dynasty's *Taotie* (a mythical ferocious animal) image and Kuilong (one-legged monster in a fable) dragon pattern, took the dominant theme. Bronze ware in this period is regarded as the transformation from the Shang to Zhou in quality and style, highlighting its style and features of the time. However, the decline of the state power and the patriarchal clan system also had a negative influence to the ritual ware, resulting in a pervasive poor production.

At the end of the Western Zhou Dynasty, society was under intense turmoil with fierce internal and external contradictions. The Zhou court lost its influence and authority, which led to its demise. Although bronze ware cast in this period showed a last brilliance with some famous heavy ware and long inscriptions with immense historic value, the impression of them to the later generations was an illusion due to the weak economy, spiritual strength and the previous efforts in craftsmanship improvement.

Bronze Ware in the Eastern Zhou Dynasty

The Eastern Zhou Dynasty witnessed the second peak in the development of bronze ware in China.

After the fall of the Western Zhou, the new successor Emperor Pingwang, in 700 BC, was forced to abandon the original capital Haojing and moved it to Luoyi (today's Luoyang, Henan), marking the start of the Eastern Zhou. Consisting of the Spring and Autumn Period (770–476 BC) and the Warring States Period (475–221 BC), the Eastern Zhou Dynasty experienced intense social turmoil and was called an age of "collapsed ritualism and music system." During this period, the Zhou's imperial reign declined and nobles contended for hegemony, resulting in years of conflict and economic centers relocating to kingdoms. "Contention of a hundred schools of thought" appeared in ideological circles. Confucianism, Taoism, and the school of Mohist, Legalists, Logicians and Naturalists created several controversies in philosophy, politics and other respects, having significant influence on culture and art at that time.

New reforms challenged the original ritual and musical system. Bronze ware, the physical carrier of "ritualism," was also changed. Although bronze ritual and musical instruments were paid special attention as the symbol of power and wealth in the noble and upper class, profound changes had taken place in the following two aspects.

The first change was the arrogation of the old system. The *Ding* application system was stringently regulated with the patriarchal clan system and hierarchy in the Western Zhou was broken and changed. This phenomena were proven by the unearthed bronze *Ding* from the tombs of some nobles of the Eastern Zhou. Generally, two sets of hierarchy-indicator *Ding* were applied for a higher level. For instance, nobles, normally applying seven *Ding*, used nine *Ding*, the qualification of the emperor, which was forbidden in the Western Zhou. It was the same for musical instruments. For example, Ji Huanzi of the Lu Kingdom employed the dance routine of the emperor in his ancestral temple. The contemporaneous Confucius (572–479 BC) scolded him, saying: "If it can be stood, whatever can't be stood?"

Warring States Period. Zenghou Yi Tomb Jiangu Bronze Stand 50cm high. It was excavated from the Zenghou Yi tomb, Suixian county, Hubei in 1978. Kept in Hubei Museum.

Warring States Period. Hollow *Ding* with *Panchi* Pattern
50cm high. Unearthed from Liuquan, Xinjiang county, Shanxi Province in 1980. Kept in Shanxi Archeology Research Institute.
The vessel has two layers. The outer layer is hollow, consisting of a snarled Panchi pattern for decoration.

Second, the change in shape, adornment and pattern showed bronze ware switched to have living and practical use. The function of ware for sacrifices, rites and music systems faded out, while the practical demand led the direction of bronze ware production. Bronze ware steadily evolved to become the deluxe utensils in nobles' luxury banquets to the divine ware for offering sacrifice to ancestors. Various gorgeous bronze ware in the Shang and Western

Warring States. Figure-shaped Bronze Lamp
21.3cm high. Unearthed from Zhucheng, Shandong Province in 1957. Kept in the National Museum of China.

Warring States Period. Tiger Eating
Deer Screen Stand with Inlaid Gold
and Silver Wire
21.9cm high, 51cm long and weighs
26.65kg. Excavated from the tomb of
the King of the Zhongshan Kingdom,
Pingshan county, Hebei Province in
1977. Kept in Hebei Cultural Relics
Research Institute.

Zhou dynasties were replaced by wooden ware, while musical
instruments, carriages and mirrors and other routine necessities
of nobles were greatly developed. The consecutive wars among
kingdoms also drove the development of bronze weapons,
resulting in great varieties and quantities. Some weapons are
deemed as art due to their fine craftsmanship.

With the decline of the Zhou court and the emergence of
kingdoms, bronze ware casting scattered into various kingdoms.
From the beginning of the Spring and Autumn Period, under
the unified times style, bronze art in Sanjin, Qilu, Yandai, Qin,
Wuyue, Xuchu and other kingdoms forged their own regional
features. The bronze art in the southern Chu Kingdom had the
biggest impact in the Warring States Period.

In the Eastern Zhou Dynasty, the scale and technology of

Warring States Period. Dragon and Phoenix Square Pattern
36.2cm high, 47.5cm long and weighs 18.65kg. Unearthed from the tomb of the King
of Zhongshan Kingdom, Pingshan county, Hebei in 1977. Kept in Hebei Cultural Relics
Research Institute.

bronze ware made a huge leap.

In bronze smelting, people had an in-depth understanding of bronze material through long-term practice. According to the Record of Kaogong, the Rites of Zhou, the Qi's government summarizes the alloy proportions of copper and stannum (plumbum) in six different bronze wares. When making bells and the *Ding*, the weight of the stannum is one-sixth to that of the copper. When making axes and tools, the weight of the stannum is one-fifth to that of the copper. When making weapons, the proportion of the stannum should be increased for high tenacity. The weight of the stannum is one-quarter to that of the copper for halberds and the like, and one-third for broadswords. But if the stannum proportion is excessive, it will be brittle and not

Warring States Period. Bronze Lying Deer
52cm high, 26.4cm long. Excavated from Sanlidun, Lianshui, Jiangsu in 1965. Kept in Nanjing Museum.
When it was unearthed, a bronze mirror was attached. Thus it must be a mirror stand.

firm any more. Thus, the 50-50 copper and stannum proportion is only suitable for making bronze and ignition mirrors. This theory shows the progress of the technology as the earliest copper making experience in the world's science history.

As early as in the Erlitou Culture Period, people were able to separately cast the main parts and accessories and then mold them together. In the middle of the Spring and Autumn Period, the main parts and accessories could be separately cast and then welded together, showing high efficiency, as well as the promotion of products with fixed specifications and a more flexible processes for complicated shapes. The establishment of the wax-loss process drove bronze ware casting technology to its peak. The wax-loss process is also known as mold-melting foundry. First, beeswax and eutexia materials were used to make molds, then covering the surface, then after a shell was hardened, heating it again to melt the wax out and form a mold cavity, and finally pouring melted copper into it to make a mold. The advantages of the process are high precision and integrated molding instead of separate processes. It is suitable for casting components for sophisticated items.

Ancient craftspeople, unsatisfied with the single appearance of bronze ware, attempted to endow them with rich colors or changes in layers. Bronze ware found in Erlitou Culture Site applied jade inlay techniques, which was popularly employed in the Shang Dynasty. After the middle Spring and Autumn Period, gold, silver, other metals, jade and colored glaze inlay started to become pervasive and reached their heyday in the Warring States Period. Gold and silver inlay refers to embedded gold or silver wires and slices into the prefabricated grooves on the bronze ware and then ground to make it secure. The gold and silver wires on some ware are as fine as hairs, which are lines carved with blades filled with gold and silver. The gold and silver inlay ware was often adorned with turquoise or other lustrous and colorful materials, increasing the artistic charm through color contrasts.

The aim of the changes and technological improvement of the bronze ware production led to the change of aesthetic trends in the Eastern Zhou Dynasty, especially in the Warring Period. The Eastern Zhou pursued a rich variety, large volume, sophisticated and exquisite process skills, showing an unprecedented gorgeous and brilliant showcase. However, the change caused the loss of the essential meaning of bronze ware in the Xia, Shang and Western Zhou dynasties, signifying the splendid art of bronze approaching its end.

The World of Bronze Ware

A ncient bronze ware is classified into utensils, wine vessels, water containers, instruments and weapons in accordance with their functions and shapes.

Bronze Utensils

Bronze utensils, belonging to ritual ware, were mainly used in sacrifices, banquets and other ceremonies or events for cooking and holding meat, millets, broomcorn millets, rice and sorghum, and so on. Different utensils represented different ranks and the hierarchy of the users.

Ding

The *Ding*, as a core bronze ritual ware among various bronze ware, is one of the main elements in sacrifices, court activities, banquets, funerals and other events.

According to their functions, the *Ding* is further categorized into *Huo Ding, Sheng Ding* and *Xiu Ding* (also called "Auxiliary *Ding*") for cooking animal sacrificial meat, holding the cooked meat and the seasoning soup. *Sheng Ding*, also known as the Main *Ding*, represents the noble identity.

According to the popular historical story of *"Chu Wang Wen Ding,"* in 606 BC, King Zhuangwang of the Chu State started a war to attack the Rong State controlled by Lu Hun. King Zhuangwang stationed his army at the border when passing the Eastern Zhou's capital Luo Yi and sent envoys to ask about the weight of the nine *Ding* stored in the court. The Emperor of Zhou sent his minister Wang Sunman for a reply. He said at the time of the establishment of the Xia Dynasty, the ruler of nine regions paid bronze as tribute to cast the nine *Ding* with various images engraved on them to tell the people how to achieve auspiciousness and avoid omnipotence. The nine *Ding* of the Xia were passed to the Shang and Zhou dynasties and protected by those with virtues and capabilities. Although the Zhou Dynasty declined, the will of Heaven was unchanged, and so one must not ask about the weight of the nine *Ding*.

Ancient literature has written that, besides the King Zhuangwang of the Chu State, the Qin and Qi States also asked about the nine *Ding* in the Zhou Dynasty. But they were also stalled by eloquent ministers. It is said that the nine *Ding* were captured by the King of the Qing State and eventually disappeared.

The legend on the nine *Ding* was mysterious and vague, but the following two points are clear.

First, *Ding*-related vocabulary definitely points to the state regime. For instance, setting the *Ding*, means the establishment of political power. *Ding* move means the transfer of the state regime. Asking for the *Ding* means the ambition to the regime. *Ding Zuo*, similar to *Guo Zuo*, means the duration of a state.

Second, the diction of the *Nine Ding* mainly appeared in the literature of the Eastern Zhou and the later dynasties, indicating a production during the Zhou Dynasty since the Xia and Shang dynasties had no ritualism on the nine *Ding*. Thus, without a doubt, the *Ding* is a symbol of state power.

In primitive society, the *Ding* is a kind of ordinary cooking vessel baked with clay. The main part is a pot, basin or similar containers standing on three legs for heating. At the end of the primitive society, the process of making some clay *Ding* improved. The size was enlarged as the practical function faded out. Bronze *Ding* made a debut in the slave society. The evolvement from clay *Ding* to bronze *Ding* does not simply mean material and technology progress. Instead, it was an essential change of social significance and spiritual connotation conveyed by the *Ding*.

The reason for the bronze *Ding* representing state power lies at the owner's special power in casting bronze ware for sacrifices and the position of the owner.

In order to make the viewers feel the owner's stable and unshakable power, the shape of the bronze ware must be flawless and rigidly symmetric, which is not easy to achieve. Round body bronze *Ding* at the early time of the Shang Dynasty were quite

Shang. *Simuwu Ding*
133cm high in total, spout 110cm long, 79cm wide, and weighs 832.84kg. Unearthed from Wuguan village, Anyang, Henan in 1939. Kept in the National Museum of China.
In the belly wall are inscribed three Chinese characters "Si Mu Wu." It is the largest bronze ware known so far.

flawless in shape but unsymmetrical. The ears were symmetrical but the legs were not when viewed from the front. Later, artisans improved the molding through adding a triangular bottom mould. Thus the symmetry difficulty of ears and legs were solved, and the problem of hollow legs was overcome as well.

Volume was an important way to be visually shocking. To date, the largest bronze ware cast in the three dynasties was Simuwu Square *Ding*, a ritual ware cast during the reign of Emperor Wen *Ding* in the Shang Dynasty as a sacrifice for his mother Wu (Wuyi's wife). The square *Ding*, 133cm-high, 110cm-broad in mouth and 79cm-wide, weighs 832.4kg and has four column-like legs, showing a solemn and majestic architectural beauty with its

Shang. *Duling* Square *Ding*
100cm high. Unearthed from Zhengzhou, Henan Province in 1974. Kept in the National Museum of China.
It was an important ritual object of the early Shang Dynasty.

enormous volume and grandness.

To strengthen the visual effect of magnificence, the designer made great improvements in overall proportion and detail treatment. The previous *Ding*, like the Duling Square *Ding*, cast under the early Shang court's supervision and unearthed in Zhengzhou, Henan, also looks grand and solemn. However, it is not comparable with the Simuwu *Ding*. The 100cm-high Duling Square *Ding*, with a deep belly and short legs looking like a mallet, seems like a bigheaded, stout child. The Simuwu *Ding*, square in shape with the proper proportion of ears and legs, looks like an adult. In the aspect of detail treatment, the rim and the external side of the ears of Duling Square *Ding* are thin, while the Simuwu *Ding* has thicker ears and rim. In the aspect of adornment, the Simuwu *Ding* has a large space in the center of the four sides with mysterious Taotie and Kuilong designs. On the external sides of both ears, a pair of horrible relief tigers stand opposite with a head inside each of their open jaws. The picture is also found in the Shang's weapon Fuhao Battle-ax, a special weapon of high-level nobles. A view from any angle to the Simuwu *Ding* will give a feeling of terror due to its mysterious and eerie images.

Shang. Man-face Square *Ding*
38.5cm high. Unearthed from Huangcun Village, Ningxiang, Hunan Province in 1959. Kept in Hunan Museum.

The square *Ding*, as a unique type of bronze ware, has no clay models. Similar works of the Shang Dynasty also include Human Face Square *Ding* unearthed in Ningxiang, Hunan, Simuxi Square *Ding*, Ox Square *Ding* and Deer Square *Ding* unearthed from the tombs of nobles in the Yin ruins, Anyang. Each of the

Western Zhou. *Yu Ding*
101.9cm high, and weighs 153.5kg.
It was excavated from Licun Village,
Qishan, Shaanxi Province in the 29th
year of Emperor Daoguang (1849) of
the Qing Dynasty. Kept in the National
Museum of China.

four sides of the Human Face Square *Ding* has a huge relief of a human face in realism. But it is not a human being with horns and claws. It is the only bronze ware with a human face as the adornment. Some one guessed the image was related with the legend of the "Four-face Huangdi."

Square *Ding* were still pervasive in the early Zhou Dynasty, but no longer had the majestic structure like the Simuwu *Ding* in the Shang Dynasty. The small volume and fine fabrication of these *Ding* are more exquisite but less majestic than those made in the Shang Dynasty. Round *Ding* were more pervasive in the period, especially the heavy and enormous round *Ding*. Yu *Ding*, cast in the beginning of the Zhou Dynasty, is the most famous one of them.

Yu *Ding*, 101.9cm-long, is round and plump with two ears sticking out, resulting in a harmonious and clear contour line. The rim is curled inward and is adorned with a Taotie image, repeating the upper relief Taotie design. The belly is smooth without any adornment. The 291-character inscription on the Yu *Ding* records the emperor awarded 1,708 people to Yu and warned him not to handle the administrative issues when drunk in the 23rd year reign of Emperor Kangwang of the Zhou Dynasty (997 BC). The inscription on the Yu *Ding* is of high value to academics specializing in the Western Zhou Dynasty.

Some famous big *Ding* cast in the Western Zhou Dynasty,

Spring and Autumn Period. Wangziwu *Ding*
69cm high, spout diameter 66cm, and weighs 100.2kg. It was unearthed from Xiasi,
Xichuan, Henan Province in 1978. Kept in Henan Museum.
It is the largest of seven Ding unearthed at the same time. On the inner wall there are 84
Chinese characters, recording that Wangziwu made the vessel during the reign of the King
Chukangwang. Wangziwu was son of King Chuzhuangwang.

such as De *Ding* and Dake *Ding* are preserved in the Shanghai
Museum and Chunhua *Ding* collected in the Shaanxi History
Museum, inherited and developed the shape of Yu *Ding*.

At the end of the Western Zhou Dynasty, the round belly
Ding were gradually replaced by half-moon and horse shoe-
shape *Ding* with Maogong *Ding* and Song *Ding* as key examples.
Maogong *Ding*, cast during the reign of Emperor Xuanwang of
the Zhou Dynasty (827–781 BC), is preserved in the National
Palace Museum, Taipei. The 499-character inscription represents
the Zhou court's appointment to Maogong Cuo. The *Ding* is well
proportioned and simply adorned with only one ring and one
string pattern, indicating the elegance and harmony of the bronze
ware in the Western Zhou Dynasty.

Warring States Period. *Ding* with Spout with Gold and Silver Wire Inlaid Flower Patterns 11.4cm high. Excavated from Xiaotun, Luoyang, Henan Province in 1981. Kept in Luoyang Cultural Relics Work Team of Henan Province.

The quantity and size of *Ding* applications were rigidly restrained by rituals in the Western Zhou Dynasty, such as the Lie *Ding* system. The Emperor can use nine, nobles seven, scholar officials, five and the scholar, three. In important sacrifices, various *Ding* are ranked in order with ox, sheep, pig and fish inside it.

After the Eastern Zhou Dynasty, the *Ding* application system ended due to the collapse of the ritual and music system. The shape of the *Ding* focused more on practical use and diversification. For instance, adding lids to keep things at a certain temperature; changing the design of the ears for the convenience of lifting; and, applying deep-belly and round bottom shapes for the *Ding* used for cooking meat.

The series of *Ding* unearthed from the tombs of nobles of the Chu Kingdom and other kingdoms deeply influenced by the Chu's culture clearly represent the development trend of bronze *Ding* in that period. For example, the Sheng *Ding* (formal *Ding*) range unearthed from the early Warring State's Zenghou Yi's tomb, consisting of nine pieces, has an open mouth, thick square rim, shallow belly, slim waist, two outward-protruding ears and horse shoe-shaped short legs supporting a flat belly. Shiny turquoise is inlaid in the body with four dragons as adornments. Straight-line structures are mostly applied with diversified adornments and patterns for decorative enrichment. It looks grand from far away and magnificent from nearby, showcasing the romance of the Chu culture. Wangzi Wu *Ding*, excavated from the Xia Temple, Xichuan, Henan and Zenghou Yi *Ding* is a typical piece of Chu's Sheng *Ding*.

Some small *Ding* cast in the Warring States Period focused on exquisite and gorgeous design and proper functions. For instance, the 11.4cm-high Cuojin Yunwen *Ding*, unearthed in Xianyang, Shaanxi, is stout, eared and spouted, equipped with a ring on the lid and completely decorated with gold and silver-wire inlaid pattern of a lotus flower, triangle and clouds. It is both a practical and an exquisite work.

A piece of *Ding* made in the Qin Dynasty was found in a pit at the side of the tomb of Emperor Qinshihuang. Even though the lid was lost, the weight of the *Ding*'s body is still about 212kg. The *Ding*'s pattern is magnificent and gorgeous but the grandness of the *Ding* in the Shang and Zhou dynasties has disappeared.

Gui

The *Gui* is a food vessel for holding broomcorn millets, millets and other food.

It is simple in style and is from the Shang Dynasty. It looks like a deep-belly bowl, with ears on both sides for lifting and loop

Western Zhou. *Li Gui*
28cm high, spout diameter 22cm, and weighs 7.95kg. Excavated from Lintong, Shaanxi Province in 1976. Kept in Lintong County Museum.
The vessel has an inscription of 32 Chinese characters and was an important vessel of the early Western Zhou Dynasty.

legs below for support and stability.

In the Western Zhou Dynasty, the *Gui* started to be used in odd numbers with *Ding* in even numbers. For instance, the emperor uses nine *Ding* with eight *Gui*, and nobles use seven *Ding* with six *Gui*. The integration of different-sized *Ding* with an equivalent-volume *Gui* presents unity amid change.

With the increasing importance of *Gui* in ceremonies, the quantity greatly increased and the shapes were enriched. Some were added with lids, some with pendants, some with beasts' heads, some with three beast legs or a square seat attached to the hoop leg, resulting in a grand effect.

Hu Gui, cast in the 12th year of the reign of Emperor Liwang of the Zhou Dynasty (865 BC), measuring 59cm in height and 60kg in weight, was the largest copper *Gui* in size known today. The inscription is the address made by Emperor Liwang to offer sacrifices to previous emperors. Hu *Gui* has a large mouth and body. Direct patterns are decorated on the belly and the square seat. Curled designs are adorned on the rim and hoop legs. Two highly placed ears are hollowed out into a dragon's head shape with a Kuilong pendant, showing a spreading force to the surroundings.

Western Zhou. *Hu Gui*
59cm high, spout diameter 43cm, belly 23cm deep, and weighs 60kg. Unearthed from Famen town, Fufeng, Shaanxi Province in 1978. Kept in Fufeng Museum. The lid and the vessel share the same inscription of 112 Chinese characters. It was important vessel of the late Western Zhou imperial family.

The ware showcases grandeur and majesty but lacks prudence, indicating the decline of the Western Zhou's economy.

The *Gui* was still popular in the Spring and Autumn Period with less changes in shape. After the Warring Period, the shape of the *Gui* tended to become simple and convenient. The *Gui* gradually lost its original appearance and was replaced by other vessels.

Xu, Fu, Dui

During the late Western Zhou Dynasty, *Xu* and *Fu*, which evolved from *Gui*, were vessels used for holding broomcorn millets, millets, rice and sorghums.

Xu, evolving from *Gui*, has a lid and an oval belly. It can be placed backwards since the lid has different square legs. Tile designs were applied as decoration on the belly. After a short period popularity, *Xu* disappeared in the early Spring and Autumn Period.

Fu, possibly imitating wooden and bamboo ware, largely applied

Western Zhou. Lubo Yu *Xu*
19.2cm high, spout 23.5cm long, 15.2cm wide.
Excavated from the ancient city of the Luo Kingdom, Qufu, Shandong Province in 1977. Kept in Qufu Cultural Relics Administration Committee.
The lid and vessel body share the same inscription of 36 Chinese characters in six lines, recording that Lubo Yu made the vessel for his parents.

Western Zhou. Bronze *Fu*
17.3cm high. Unearthed from Guantaizi, Lixin county, Anhui Province in 1984. Kept in Lixin County Cultural Relics Administration.

Spring and Autumn Period. *Dui*
Embedded with Dragon Pattern
33cm high, spout diameter 22cm.
Excavated from Shouxian county, Anhui Province in 1955. Kept in Anhui Museum.

straight-line design, and the body is square. The slanting lines on the walls extend outside like rays. Ring-type ears are on both sides with hoop legs on the bottom. The lid matches the body properly with only a subtle clip at the joint. Rigid square *Fu* and other round bronze ware are in a set, indicating both unification and change and showcasing diverse bronze ritual ware shapes.

Dui mainly pervaded in the Eastern Zhou Dynasty. It has various shapes. The most typical one is a combination of two half-moons with hoop ears on both sides and straight legs. If divided in half, they are two of the same vessels. The Inlaid Triangle Cloud Pattern Dui in the Shanghai Museum is embedded with turquoise and silver and cooper wires, showing a splendid look.

Li, Yan

Li and *Yan* are also important bronze utensils.

Li, a cooking vessel for food, is generally believed for cooking congee, or rice porridge. According to archeological study, *Li* was also used in cooking or holding meat since pig bones were found in *Li*. It looks like a *Ding*. The belly and three legs created a hollow bag-like space, called *"Kuanzu"* in design, which helped to enlarge the heating area and shorten cooking times.

Li, started from early Shang until the Warring States Period, was pervasive after the middle

Western Zhou. Boju *Li*
33cm high. Unearthed from Fangshan county, Beijing in 1975. Kept in the Capital Museum.
The vessel has an inscription of 15 Chinese characters in four lines.

period of the Western Zhou Dynasty. Some *Li* made in Western Zhou were gorgeous, like the *Boju Li*, unearthed in Liuli River, Fangshan, Beijing, has a top lid and a belly with relief ox head and protruding horns. Two ox heads on opposite sides of the lid were used as the handles.

Yan, a vessel for braising and boiling, consists of *Zeng* as the upper part and Li as the lower part for holding food and water with a screen in between for steaming. Bronze *Yan* first appeared in the middle of the Shang Dynasty, and were used up until the late Warring States Period. It is round and square in shape and not many exist. Enormous *Yan* were also found, for example, the Standing Deer *Yan* with Beast-adorned Ears unearthed in a tomb of a noble in the Shang Dynasty in Dayangzhou, Xingan, Jiangxi, measuring 105cm in height, has four legs with relief oxen heads as adornments on each side. Double layer swallow

Shang. *Yan* with an animal face pattern and deer standing on the legs
105cm high, vessel mouth diameter 61.2cm, *Ge*39.5cm high. Unearthed from Dayangzhou, Xingan county, Jiangxi Province in 1989. Kept in Jiangxi Museum.

tail patterns were applied on both ears with two small beasts standing on them.

Utensils for holding meat pastes and pickled vegetables had been pervasive in the Western and Eastern dynasties. One type is the disk-like *Pu* with a high seat and a lid. The other is *Dou* with a half-moon like belly and a long handle and hoop legs.

Bronze Wine Vessels

Ancient Chinese learned the art of brewery very early. Archeologists discovered the components of ancient wine featuring rice, honey, fruit and barley through the analysis of pottery of Longshan Culture in the late Neolithic Age.

According to ancient literature, traders enjoyed drinking. Emperor Zhouwang of the Shang Dynasty even built a wine pond and meat mountain for dining and wining day and night. Under such social customs, bronze wine vessels were quite developed in the Shang Dynasty, becoming the most important ware for sacrificing deities and ancestors.

In the early period of the Western Zhou, the emperor, taking into consideration that excessive drinking in the Shang Dynasty caused early deaths, gave the order for prohibition during routine life. Thus, the quantity and variety of bronze wine vessels in the Western Zhou greatly dropped. Food vessels instead became the dominant bronze ware in the Western Zhou instead of wine vessels in the Shang Dynasty. However, wine vessels were important ritual ware for that period.

There are various wine vessels and simply classified into two categories for easy identification. One is called hoop-legged ware, the other is named three-legged ware. Functionally, they can be categorized into wine vessels for drinking, heating, holding and blending.

Longshan Culture
Longshan Culture is a general term to the cultural relics of the late Neolithic Age in the middle and lower reaches of the Yellow River. It was named Longshan Culture because it was discovered in Chengziya Relics, Longshan Town, Zhangqiu, Shandong province in 1928. It was also named Black Pottery Culture because inky and bright black pottery and black thin-wall shell pottery were common in the relics. Longshan Culture can be seen in the wide area of middle and lower reaches of the Yellow River, but featuring different cultural connotations and sources. As a matter of fact, it is not a single portion of archaeological culture. Generally, Longshan Culture was in the period of the patrilineal society.

Gu, Zhi

Gu, a general hoop leg wine beaker, connects the trumpet-like mouth with the hoop leg with a short cylindrical belly. The part above the belly was used for steady placement, showcasing a straight and slender image.

The shape of bronze *Gu* borrowed the inspiration of the pottery *Gu* in primitive society. Early ones were stout, and its shape was greatly improved through constant development after the middle period of the Shang Dynasty. The spout is adorned with a banana leaf pattern with an outward expansion effect. The arris of the *Gu*

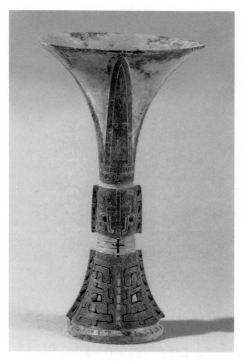

Shang. Huang *Gu*
27.3cm high, and weighs 1.4kg. Kept in Shanghai Museum.

Western Zhou. *Fugeng Zhi*
14.9cm high, spout diameter 7.6cm, bottom diameter 5.1cm, 340g heavy. Kept in Shanghai Museum.

were applied on the peripheral to show a colored and beautiful contour. The constant and diversified contour line continued to the vessel's bottom, forming a powerful square arris.

In total, 53 pieces of *Gu*, boasting the largest number of all kinds of bronze wine vessels in one place, were unearthed from the Fuhao tomb of the Shang Dynasty. Different shapes and proper proportions displayed the designers' and makers' workmanship.

After the Eastern Dynasty, the Qi'er beaker replaced the bronze *Gu*, arousing Confucius' lament of "*Gu* does not looks like a *Gu*. How can it be called *Gu* any more?" It also reflected the downfall of ritual and musical practice.

Zhi, similar to *Gu* in shape, is smaller in volume and lower for the center of gravity. The upper part expands outward, the middle part narrows while the lower part is shaped like an egg with a short hoop leg for support, creating a beautiful image.

Zun

Zun, *Lei* and *You* are all large wine-holding vessels derived from *Gu*-like hoop-legged vessels.

Zun, with a shape similar with *Gu*, has a large volume and features two basic patterns, square and round. The features of Zun were defined very early. Dragon and Tiger Zun, Four-goat Square *Zun* and other successful works were made in the Shang Dynasty. The shape and design primarily took the practical function into consideration and strengthen its spiritual influence in the detail process.

Four-goat Square *Zun*, unearthed in Ningxiang, Hunan, measuring 58.3cm in height, 52.4cm in spout length and 34.5kg in weight, is a masterpiece of square *Zun* due to its grandeur and majesty. The upper part has eight ridges extending to the rim, responding to the square shape at the bottom, showing a grand and solemn visual effect.

The shoulder and belly parts of the Four-goat Square *Zun* are most vivid. Each of the four sides of the belly has a big horn-curled goat. The goats' heads are protruding, and the curled horns enrich the three-dimensional effect of the design. The goats' shoulders are adorned with bird patterns, and the hoofs are cast with the hoop leg. Although each goat is only half outlined, the combination of goats gives a complete impression. Each side of the shoulder of the *Zun* has a dragon, with a dragon's head at the joint part of two goats, showing variations among integration.

Dragon-Tiger *Zun*, unearthed in Funan, Anhui, is a typical round *Zun* with a big spout, wide shoulder and high hoop leg. Different with the fine patterns on the Four-goat Square *Zun*, the upper part is smooth with only three protruding string patterns on the neck to respond to the upper string pattern. A half-moon

Shang. Four-goat Square *Zun*
58.3cm high, spout 52.4cm
long, and weighs 34.5kg.
Excavated from Yueshanpu,
Ningxiang, Hunan Province
in 1938. Kept in the National
Museum of China.

arc starts from the rim, changes to a bow-shaped arc at the shoulder part and then the hoop leg steadily supports the body, indicating a nice contour with abundant internal strength.

The shoulder and belly are the most wonderful parts of the Dragon-Tiger *Zun*. At the shoulder, there are three relief dragons with protruding heads as the adornments for the sacrificial ware. The belly under the dragons' heads is divided into three independent parts with one head and two tigers on each part. The tigers hold nude tattooed figures with curled arms and legs in the animals' mouths. Reversed *Kuilong* are on both sides of the figures and combined with the neighboring *Kuilong* into a *Taotie*

Shang. Dragon-Tiger *Zun* 50.5cm high, spout diameter 44.7cm, and weighs about 20kg. Unearthed from Funan, Anhui Province in 1957. Kept in the National Museum of China.

pattern. If the *Zun* is turned 90 degrees, the upper dragons' heads and the lower *Taotie* pattern become the obverse decoration and the protruding tiger heads the accessory adornments. The exquisite design indicates that bronze smiths in the Shang Dynasty paid great attention to the appreciation effect from multiple angles.

The Zenghou Yi *Zun Pan* in the early period of the Warring States is the most sophisticated and complicated one. It was in the *Pan* (tray) when unearthed, and also called *Pan Zun*. The body applies oval casting and the spout uses the lost wax method to produce hollow accessory adornments. The inner layer applies a hollow network structure, and the outer layer uses copper

Warring States Period. Zenghou Yi *Zun Pan*
The *Zun* is 30.1cm high, while the *Pan* is 23.5cm high. Unearthed from the tomb of Zenghou Yi, Suixian, Hubei Province in 1978. Kept in Hubei Museum.

wires to connect with each other, forming a vivid *Panhui* (lizard) pattern. Looking from the spout, it seems like a beautiful solid flower ring. Multiple solid adornments are attached to the *Zun* with four dragon-shaped ears on the neck and four two-bodied lively dragons on the belly and legs welded to the body. The *Pan,* using the same cast process with the *Zun,* applies the combination and overlapping different-sized dragon-shaped pieces, showing an intense visually shocking appearance. The casting technology was too sophisticated to be achieved by the later generations.

The Zenghou Yi *Zun Pan,* as the fruit of numerous masters' efforts, embodies the new achievements of the Warring States Period. However, artistically, it seems a little complicated and impractical.

Lei, You

Lei, coordinating with *Zun* in application, has a similar design with *Zun*. Zun has an open spout, while the Lei a small spout with a lid for holding wine without volatility. The Lei has a wide shoulder and narrow bottom with a hoop leg to keep a steady position after it is filled with wine. Both sides of the shoulder have two beasts' head ears, and the beast's nose is like a button installed on the bottom of the belly, for the convenience of binding and lifting.

In the Shang and Zhou dynasties, some of *Lei* are beautiful, and some are plain. Dragon lid and beast face *Lei* unearthed in Kazuo, Liaoning and Pengxian, Sichuan is elegant and dignified. The round carved dragon on the lid, turned back to look at from behind, is very lively. The shoulder part is decorated with a typical *Kuilong* design popular in the Western Dynasty.

You, was an article for holding *Juchang*, a kind of valuable wine brewed from black millet and vanilla. Four sides of *You* are installed with rods for lifting. It had many varieties in the Shang Dynasty. Some are square, round, oval, cylindrical or bird- and beast-like. Round neck and square belly *You* with a crossing hole in the

Western Zhou. *Lei* with Dragon Lid and Animal Face Pattern
44.5cm high, spout diameter 15.3cm. Excavated from Beidong, Kazuo county, Liaoning Province in 1973. Kept in Liaoning Museum.

Shang. Bronze Square *You* with Cross-shaped Hole
27.8cm high. Unearthed from Dayangzhou, Xingan county,
Jiangxi Province in 1989. Kept in Jiangxi Museum.

belly were also found. *You* and *Zun* were used together in the Western Zhou, starting with one *Zun* and two *You* set to one *Zun* and one *You* set.

Kettle

The kettle, sometimes deemed a water vessel, was a kind of important hoop-leg wine vessel. There was a large number and variety shapes. The early kettle, referring to the shape of *Zhi* and *You*, is slender in shape with the center of gravity at the center of the belly. After the middle period of the Western Zhou Dynasty, the shape changed, showing a long neck, round belly and the downward center of gravity.

A pair of Xing Kettles, unearthed in Fufeng, Shaanxi made in middle Western Zhou, can hold a large volume and are elegant in shape. The neck is slender. The center of gravity of the kettle is at the lower belly. The top lid and the lower hoop leg respond with each other in shape. Three layers of smooth and broad ripple patterns are adorned on the body under the backdrop of cloud patterns. It looks solemn and lively in appearance. The shape and designs have profound influences on the fine arts of the later generation. For example, the shape of the porcelain of Jade Kettle Spring Vase and garlic-shape vase may be sourced back to the Xing Kettle.

Song Kettle (made by Song craftsman) is a representative of the popular kettles in the Western Zhou. There are only

Western Zhou. Three-year Xing Kettle 65.4cm high, and weighs 25.5kg. Excavated from Fufeng county, Shaanxi Province in 1976. Kept in Zhouyuan Cultural Relics Administration. On the outer surface of the lid there are 60 Chinese characters in 12 lines, recording that the noble Xing was awarded in the third year feasting rites of the Emperor of Zhou Dynasty and made the vessel for ancestral sacrifices.

two existing Song Kettles, one in the National Museum of China and the other in the National Palace Museum, Taipei. The Song Kettle has a square shape and round corners, indicating the same design concept with Xing Kettle. Its eye-catching features are four one-headed and two-bodied dragons surrounding the ware with ripple patterns on the neck, showing a harmonious design combination. Some square kettles in the late Zhou Dynasty are similar with the Song Kettle in shape. But a range of ribbon-like mountain shapes was designed on the lid. Some were hollowed for a transparent and hollow effect.

Spring and Autumn Period. Standing Crane Square Kettle
126cm high, and weighs 64.28kg. Unearthed in a pair from Lijialou, Xinzheng, Henan Province. Kept in the Palace Museum and Henan Museum.

Lengthy inscriptions of regular characters were cast on kettles, Song Kettles and other ware, indirectly reflected its important position in grand ceremonies.

After the Spring and Autumn Period, kettles tended to be complicated and noble. A pair of Standing Crane Square Kettles, unearthed in Xinzheng, Henan, are pioneering work in art vogue. The big kettle is full of dragon and phoenix relief patterns and solid adornments on the surface. On the lid, a crane stands on a two-layered lotus flower. The crane is completely realistic, showing a fresh and nice image under the backdrop of eerie and mysterious designs. Two small beasts are crawling to support the hoop leg of the kettle. The beasts look aside and make faces. It seems that the 64.28kg kettle they are carrying is very light.

Lianjin Kettles, unearthed from Zenghou Yi Tomb, Suixian

County, Hubei, were made in the early Warring States Period and known as the biggest bronze kettle to date. Two kettles were cast in the same *Jin* (seat), measuring 112.2cm in height and 240.2kg in weight.

Jue, Jia, He

The number of three-legged wine vessels is less than hoop-legged ones. *Jue* and *Jiao* are the main vessels for drinking and *Jia* for heating and *He* for blending.

Jue is quite beautiful in shape. The *Jue* pottery in primitive society is a direct reference for bronze *Jue* which is more delicate in detail for practical use under the precondition of full use of bronze material.

Bronze *Jue* made a debut in the Erlitou Culture Period. Erlitou was the remnant of the Xia Dynasty. The shape of the *Jue* was simple then and not harmonious in proportion. But the general shape was defined.

The belly is oval, and the mouth has a spout and tail on both sides for balance. Two small columns are erected at the joint of the back of spout and the mouth of the *Jue*. A *Pan* (handle) was placed on a side of the belly for holding. Three legs under the belly extend outward for steady standing and easy heating, showing a high-rise and upright visual effect.

Jiao, also a kind of vessel for drinking wine, came out of the basis of *Jue*. The main part of the *Jiao* is similar with the *Jue*, but not having spouts and columns.

Jia, a large vessel for warming spirits,

Shang. *Jue*
38.7cm high, 21.5cm long from the spout to the tail. Unearthed in Guanyi village, Feixi, Anhui. Kept in Anhui Museum.

can be divided into round *Jia* and square *Jia*, with an even spout, or without spout and tail. The poles on the rim are robust with a cap decoration in the shape of a mushroom, tower or umbrella. Some *Jia* are huge, for example, among the 12 bronze *Jia* unearthed from Fuhao tomb of the Shang Dynasty (1600–1046 BC), eight are 60cm high and weigh about 20kg. Some large *Jia* follows the shape of *Zun* (square wine vessel) with rods on the rim with a tower-shaped cap, and neck in the shape of robust arc. The part between *Jia* belly and the legs stretches in a straight line robustly. On the handle lies animal heads with erected ears. Generally, the *Jia* leaves a robust and powerful impression.

Shang. Fuhao Square *Jia*
68.8cm high, and weighs 18.3kg. Unearthed from the Fuhao tomb, Anyang, Henan Province in 1976. Kept in the National Museum of China.

He is an ancient utensil designed for adding water to wine to adjust the concentration of wine and for warming the beverage. Its spout is capped with a pipe-shaped spout on top or in front. The utensil has three or four legs. A *Ta He* of the late Western

Western Zhou. *Ta He*
37.5cm high. Unearthed from
Fufeng county, Shaanxi Province
in 1963. Kept in Shaanxi
Museum.

Zhou Dynasty (1046–771 BC) is very interesting: the vessel's belly is round and flat with bird-shaped cap on the top, a spout in the shape of an animal which protrudes forward, while the handle is a dragon looking back. The item has four legs in the shape of paw. The utensil is in a pose of moving forward.

Bird and animal *Zun*

The most splendid and the most mysterious bronze wine vessel of the Shang and Zhou dynasties is the ritual item named bird and animal *Zun*.

The book *Rites of Zhou* mentioned that ritual vessels used in the sacrificial activities of the ancient people consisted of "six *Zun* and six *Yi* (wine vessel)," including the chicken *Yi*, bird *Yi*, elephant *Zun* and tiger *Yi*, and so forth. There do exist bronze vessels in the shape of chicken, bird, elephant and tiger, corroborating the literature records. But the other names mentioned in the literature such as *Huang Yi* and *Shan Zun* are still unknown as to what specifically they look like despite textual research made by historical scholars. Among the unearthed bird and animal *Zun* are *Ju Zun* (colt *Zun*) and *Xi Zun* (rhinoceros *Zun*) which are not included in the literature.

Animals such as ox, sheep, pig, chicken and dog, the prototype of the bird and animal *Zun*, are the "Five Sacrifices" used in sacrificial activities in ancient times. Others such as rhinoceroses, elephants

Shang. Fuhao Xiao *Zun*
45.9cm high, and weighs 16.7kg. Excavated from the Fuhao tomb, Anyang, Henan Province in 1976. Kept in the National Museum of China.
A pair of *Zun* was unearthed. Fu Hao was inscribed inside the mouth of the vessel.

and tigers were rare animals and especially cast for presenting to deities.

The bird and animal *Zun* were popular in the Shang and Western Zhou dynasties. Some extant works were taken out of China and are currently displayed in some famous museums around the world. They feature true-life romance and can be regarded as sculpture works.

The bird *Zun* in the Shang Dynasty is mostly in the shape of a sparrow, hawk or owl, mainly unearthed from southern China such as Hunan. *Xiao Zun* follows the look of an owl with both eyes in front, symmetrical feathers growing around the eyeballs, protruding ear feathers and sharp beak. The vessel mouth is at the neck. Normally the work is decorated with images of *Taotie* (mythical ferocious animal), *Kuilong*(one-legged monster in a fable), bird and snake, and so on. Some have animal-shaped decoration at the cap or other parts acting as the handle.

A pair of *Xiao Zun,* unearthed from Fuhao tomb, Yinxu of Anyang, is quite large, 45.9cm in height. The *Zun* is in the shape of a squatted *Xiao* with its legs and tail as the support, a tall corona on the head decorated with a headstand *Kuilong* pattern. The beak is square and thick, chiseled with a cicada design on the face. There is a half-moon spout at the back of the owl's head, and a cap on which a handle was cast in the shape a *Kui* chasing after a bird. The chest of the owl is decorated with deformed bicorn cicada patterns. Both wings of the *Xiao Zun* look like a coiled snake, which is a typical form of similar works. On the top of the tail there is a high-relief owl head, below there are carved stretched wings, leaving an impression that it is flying.

Some *Xiao Zun* integrate features of other birds in different shapes. Some are standing upright proudly, some small and cute, reflecting different temperaments and

Western Zhou. Taibao Bird *You*
23.5cm high. Kept in the White Crane Art Gallery of Japan.

tastes. The patterns on the body take the shapes and poses of different creatures such as birds, animals and reptiles while adding transcendent power to the vessel. The expression technique is in line with the beliefs of the ancient people. Craftsmen used different sculpture techniques such as relief, round sculpture and line engraving skillfully and freely.

Xiao was also often used for *You* (ancient wine vessel). The *Xiao You* is often found in the shape of two *Xiao* back to back without extra decoration, rotund and lovely.

After the Western Zhou Dynasty, the bird *Zun* lost its mysterious color and tended to be lifelike. For example the duck *Zun* unearthed from Kazuo, Liaoning, completely follows the form of a fowl. The vessel is open at the back. The two wings are indicated with relief lines while the diagonal patterns outline the feathers. The *Taibao* Bird *You* collected in the White Crane Art Gallery of Japan, is in the shape of a rooster, with a long crown on its head and dewlap feather on its chin, primitive and simple.

Compared with the number of bird *Zun*, those of animal *Zun* are less. The animal *Zun* of the Shang Dynasty includes elephants, pigs, rhinoceros, tigers and ox, normally made with similar artistic expression technique with the bird *Zun* with true-life and mysterious features.

The pig *Zun* unearthed from Xiangtan, Hunan, is 40cm high and 72cm long, in the vivid shape of a boar. With a long snout and bucked teeth, its eyes are popped out forming an "E" design, and erect ears, the boar is watchful. A line of ridges indicates the boar's mane. There is a mouth on the back with a cap, on which stands a bird acting as the handle. The boar, in precise proportion and structure, boasts sturdy muscles. Even the genitals are showed clearly. However, the *Kuilong* image and cloud and lightning pattern on the body remind you it is not an ordinary animal.

A pig *You* in the Shanghai Museum is also in the shape of two

Shang. Pig *Zun*
40cm high, 72cm long, and weighs 19.25kg. Unearthed from Xiangtan, Hunan Province in 1981. Kept in Hunan Museum.

pigs standing back-to-back. The craftsman captured the moment the piglets are lowering their heads looking for food and this is vividly reflected in the image. The vessel is polished with refined decorative patterns, reflecting a high casting technique.

Artistic work on the elephant has a long history in China. In Longshan Culture Relics in Hubei, there was a ceramic elephant made during the late primitive society. The bronze elephant *Zun* existed in the Shang Dynasty.

An exquisite elephant *Zun* was unearthed in 1975 from a mountain slope of Liling, Hunan. It was only about 15cm below the surface soil. According to the archaeologists, it might have been a ritual vessel buried by the slave owner or noble during a sacrificial activity to the mountains and lakes for such a valuable ware was not unearthed from an ancestral temple or tomb but from a slope. The elephant *Zun* is massive and powerful, decorated with 11 animal patterns. The trunk rises high with the end in the shape of phoenix head, on which there is a crouching tiger, echoing with the relief of two coiling snakes on the forehead of the elephant. The detail on this part is very interesting. The spout is at the back of *Zun*, but the cap was not found. An elephant *Zun* collected in the Freer Gallery of Art and Arthur M. Sackler Gallery is similar to this one but smaller in size. On its cap there is a small elephant, which can be a reference for studying this one.

Xiaochen rhinoceros *Zun* at the Asian Art Museum of San Francisco is said to be unearthed from Liangshan, Shandong.

Shang. Liling Elephant *Zun*
22.8cm high, and 26.2cm long. Excavated from Liling, Hunan Province in 1975. Kept in Hunan Museum.

Its inscription records the history of the high level official of the Shang Dynasty who followed a king of the Shang Dynasty to attack the Fang square-state in the region. The rhinoceros *Zun* boasts a strong three-dimensional effect, representing the rhinoceros running vividly on the ground. The head skeletal structure and skin were designed with realism. The body is simple without any decoration but replete with vigor.

Shang. Xiaochen Yu Rhinoceros *Zun*
24.5cm high. It is said the vessel was excavated from Liangshan, Shouzhang county, Shandong Province. Kept in the Asian Art Museum of San Francisco.
The vessel has an inscription of 27 Chinese characters in four lines. The lid has been lost.

In the Western Zhou Dynasty, the animal *Zun* also shows obvious lifelike characteristics. For example, *Liju Zun* unearthed in Meixian county, Shaanxi province, is in the shape of a realistic colt with only two groups of simple eddy patterns on the belly of the colt. Two *Liju Zun* were made to mark the honor that *Li*, the owner of the *Zun*, participated in the ceremony of the Zhou court promoting the colt to the service horses and received an award from the emperor.

A gold wire cloud pattern

Western Zhou. Liju *Zun*
32.4cm high, 34cm long, and weighs 5.68kg. Unearthed from Licun village, Meixian county, Shaanxi Province in 1955. Kept in the National Museum of China.
The spout is on the back of the vessel with a cap. There is an inscription of nine lines, totaling 94 Chinese characters below the neck.

embedded in a rhinoceros *Zun* cast in the Warring States Period (475–221 BC) to the Western Han Dynasty was unearthed in Xingping, Shaanxi, is also a realistic work. By looking at the two horns on the rhinoceros, the researchers estimated them had African origins. The craftsman mastered the proportion of different parts precisely, especially changes of the internal skeletal structure and external muscles. The bright eyes of the rhinoceros was made of black materials and embedded. The rhinoceros are decorated with floating cloud patterns made of fine gold and sliver wires. The decoration does not distract from the whole impression, but rather enforces the sense of reality of tenacity and roughness of the skin. The spout of the *Zun* is at the back of the rhinoceros and the simple movable cap does

Warring States Period – Western Han Dynasty. Rhinoceros *Zun* with Gold Wire Inlaid Cloud Pattern
34.1cm high, 58.1cm long. Excavated from Douma village, Xingping county, Shaanxi Province in 1963. Kept in the National Museum of China.

not affect the integrity of the vessel. On both sides of the cap the leather belt type design extends to the belly of the rhinoceros. On the right side of the rhinoceros' mouth is a pipe-shaped spout leading to the belly. Though it is a lifelike work, it was designed as a wine vessel with complete functions.

Sigong, Fangyi

Among the bird and animal bronze vessels created during the Shang and Western Zhou dynasties, there is another type vessel named *Sigong* (a wine vessel). Basically it is a jar with a cap, a spout on the front and a handle on the back, with three or four ring-shaped legs. The bird and animal images such as *Xiao*, elephant, ox and tiger are formed at the cap and the vessel body together features the sculpture elements. Some *Sigong* are in the shape of an animal on the front part and a squatting *Xiao* on the rear part while some are the other way around. Some are decorated with beautiful patterns while others are very simple with little adornment.

Shang. *Gong* with Bird and Animal Patterns
31.4cm high, 31.3cm wide, and weighs 4.59kg. Kept in the Freer Gallery of Art and Arthur M. Sackler Gallery.

The *Gong* with Bird and Animal Pattern of the Shang Dynasty is collected in the Freer Gallery of Art and Arthur M. Sackler Gallery. It is decorated with more than 30 three-dimensional or relief animal patterns: the front part of the cap is an animal head while the curled horns are a pair of *Kuilong*; the rear part of the cap is a monster with fish gills and *Kui* horn. On both sides of the cap the middle part reveals a relief of *Kui*, elephant, tiger, bird and fish chasing each other. There is a big bird with a sharp beak and snake-shaped body on the front part of the vessel, while the rear area has a *Taotie*. The vessel handle is in the shape of a squatted bird. The rear legs of the four legs are the men with a serpentine body held by the *Taotie*.

Sigong was no longer made after the middle of the Western Zhou Dynasty.

Fangyi (square wine vessel) is also in relation to *Sigong*. *Fangyi* is actually a temporary name for these wine vessels made by ancient people. *Yi* is a general term of bronze ware and this wine vessel is square, and so it is called *Fangyi*. It is in the shape of a house with a cap following the shape of a roof with five ridges. Some have arc-shaped decor. Researchers speculate that the craftsmen referred to the palace buildings of that time for this design. The largest *Fangyi* is twin-*Fangyi* unearthed from the Fuhao tomb of the Shang Dynasty.

Fangyi was normally unearthed together with *Sigong*, indicating a grouping relationship between them.

Shang. Fuhao *Fangyi*
36.6cm high and weighs 10.1kg. Unearthed from the Fuhao tomb, Anyang in 1976.
Fuhao *Fangyi* is a pair in the shape of a house. Two Chinese characters are inscribed inside the cap.

Shiju Fangyi and *Li Fangyi* of the middle Western Zhou Dynasty have trunk-shaped legs on both sides with ear-shaped ornaments. A wall was built in the vessel interior, dividing the vessel into two cells for containing seasoning. There is a square opening for holding the spoon handle.

Bronze Water Vessels

The water vessel is also a kind of ritual bronze. Compared with food and wine vessels, the bronze water vessel is small in terms of type and quantity. The water vessel was mainly used for washing before and after rituals offering sacrifices to deities or ancestors and banquets, showing sincerity. The water vessel can be divided into the water injector, water-carrying vessel and water container.

Pan

Pan is a vessel used for carrying water. In the practices of offering sacrifices and banquets in the Shang and Zhou dynasties, the participant must go through the rite of washing hands, which

Western Zhou. Shiqiang *Pan*
16.2cm high, spout diameter 47.3cm, and weighs 12.5kg. Unearthed from Fufeng, Shaanxi Province in 1976. Kept in Zhouyuan Cultural Relics Administration.
At the bottom there are 284 Chinese characters in 18 lines.

stipulates pouring water onto the hands and carrying the used water with a tray. *Pan*, first seen in the early Shang Dynasty, became popular in the late Shang Dynasty and lasted until the Warring States Period.

Pan in the Shang Dynasty features a large spout, shallow belly and high ring-shaped stand, some with two legs. *Pan* was normally decorated with designs of aquatic creatures or amphibians such as fish, frogs and dragons. When the *Pan* is full of water, the images under the water will produce a vivid effect with water refraction.

Since the Zhou Dynasty some *Pan* feature long inscriptions, for example *Shiqiang Pan* (a historiographer named *Qiang*) and *Sanshi Pan* (*Shiren Pan*) and massive *Guoji Zibai Pan*. The ancient people normally "cast important documents record merits on *Pan* and *Yu* (jar)," and from that we know, *Pan* and *Yu* were important carriers of ritual ceremonies and records since the Western Zhou Dynasty.

Yi

Yi is a vase-shaped pitcher used during the hand-washing rite, normally used together with the *Pan*. A younger person carries the *Pan* to carry the used water while a senior person uses the *Yi* to pour the water in the ritual procedure. *Yi* is in the shape of *Gong* without a cap, flat and long, with a spout on the front and a handle on the rear, with four legs.

Yi emerged in the middle of the Western Zhou Dynasty, became popular later in that period and early in the

Western Zhou-the Spring and Autumn Period. Qihou *Yi* 24.7cm high, 48.1 cm long, and weighs 6.42kg. Kept in Shanghai Museum.
There are 22 Chinese characters in four lines at the bottom of the belly, recording that Qihou made the Yi for his wife Ji Liangnu, the eldest daughter of the King of the Guo Kingdom.

Warring States Period; but gradually the bronze ware started to disappear when the rite of washing hands was abandoned.

Qihou Yi, in the Shanghai Museum's collection, was made sometime in the late Western Zhou Dynasty to the Spring and Autumn Period (770–476 BC). The craftsman added parallel channel designs to the vessel according to its function, producing an impression of free flowing water. The handle is in the shape of a small dragon with the dragon's head biting the tail of *Yi*, looking like it is stretching forward to drink water. With four legs in the shape of animal paws, it like carrying *Yi* full of water and walking slowly. It is a successful model integrating design and function.

Yu

Yu is a water container with a deep belly and legs, looking like *Gui* but in a larger size. Confucius once compared the emperor to *Yu* and the people to water, and said when *Yu* was square, the water would be in the shape of square; when *Yu* was round, the water would be in a round shape. Famous *Yu* works of the Western Zhou Dynasty include *Yanhou Yu* and *Bo Yu* and so on.

Western Zhou. Yanhou *Yu* 24.5cm high, spout diameter 33.8cm, and weighs 6.45kg. Excavated from Kazuo county, Liaoning Province in 1955. It is now in the National Museum of China. Five Chinese characters were inscribed on the inner wall of the vessel, recording the event of Yanhou making the *Yu*.

Jian

Jian is a large water container, which was used to carry ice cubes. When full of water, it was also used as a mirror. That is why a mirror is also called "*Jian*." It emerged in the middle Spring and Autumn Period and became popular later in that period and the Warring States Period. *Jian* is simple in form and structure, normally large in size with a large spout, folded rim, slightly restrained neck, deep belly, even bottom or shallow ring-shaped legs, with two or four legs.

Spring and Autumn Period. Fuchai (Wu's King) *Jian* 45cm high, spout diameter 73cm, and weighs 54kg. It was said the object was excavated from Huixian, Henan Province in 1943. Kept in Shanghai Museum.
There are 13 Chinese characters in two lines, recording the event of Fuchai, the King of Wu, making the bronze *Jian*.

Fuchai (King of Wu) *Jian* of the Spring and Autumn Period unearthed in Huixian, Henan, is 45cm high, spout diameter 73cm, and decorated with splendid and detailed Panhui designs. Animal ears with rings were cast on both sides of *Jian*. On both the front and back are crouching tigers climbing up towards the rim. The image and use of the animals reflect the unique craftsmanship of the designer.

Two sets of luxury *Zenghou Yi* (fief kingdom noble named *Yi*) *Jian* and *Fou* (jar with big belly and small spout) unearthed from *Zenghou Yi* tomb, were designed especially for cooling wine, consisting of square *Jian* which carried the ice cubes and square

Warring States Period. Zenghou Yi *Jian* and *Fou*
63.2cm high, and spout diameter 63cm. Unearthed from the Zenghou Yi tomb in Suixian, Hubei Province in 1978. Kept in Hubei Museum.
It has an inscription of seven Chinese characters, recording the object was made by Zenghou Yi.

Fou which were used for carrying wine. *Jian* and *Fou* feature precise structures and splendid appearance, reflecting advanced cast techniques of that time.

Bronze Musical Instruments

The *Yue* (music) in the ancient China also refers to recreational activities including music and dance. The ancient people attached great importance to *Yue* and believed it was an expression of the rules of universal harmony. In ritual ceremonies such as offering sacrifices and banquets held by nobles were normally accompanied by *Yue*. Especially in the Western Zhou Dynasty, the *Yue* developed with the advanced ritual *Yue* system, forming a rigid but complete system. Music and dance combined with ritual activities were collectively known as "*Yayue*"(elegant music).

There were a number of musical instruments in ancient China. These musical instruments can be divided into eight categories, namely, metal, stone, earth, leather, thread, wood, gourd and bamboo, and are collectively named *Bayin* (Eight Music). Of those, metal refers to bronze musical instruments.

Small Bell

The small bell is the first bronze musical instrument found in China with many discoveries in Erlitou Cultural Relics in the late Xia Dynasty and was widely used in the Shang Dynasty. Inside the small bell there is a clapper and when the small bell is shook it will produce sound.

Nao

Nao is the first practical bronze percussion instrument of China and was first used in the late Shang Dynasty and early Western Zhou Dynasty. The instrument is in the shape of two tiles pieces without a clapper, but with a round rod named *"Yong"* (handle) on the bottom. When played, *Nao* will be placed with mouth upwards and *Yong* inserted on the wooden shelf, producing a sound when struck with a gavel.

Nao can be classified into single *Nao* and set of *Nao*, which typically consists of two, three, five or even 10 pieces of *Nao*. Different-sized *Nao* are combined to create a certain tone combination. Most of the large single *Nao* were unearthed in the southern areas

Shang. *Nao* with Animal-face Pattern
44.5cm high. Unearthed from Bojia Village, Liuyang county, Hunan Province in 1985. kept in Changsha Museum, Hunan Province.

such as Hunan, Jiangxi and Anhui provinces. A large *Nao* of the late Shang Dynasty unearthed in Hunan measures 103.5cm high, and weighs 221.5kg. The big *Nao* is normally decorated with patterns, mainly thick deformed *Taotie* designs. The large *Nao* with elephant patterns unearthed in Ningxiang, Hunan is decorated with elephants, tigers, fish and so on, and is the most beautiful and finest *Nao*.

Drum

Drums were usually made of wood. A wood drum relic with a boa skin drumhead was once found in the tombs of Yinxu, Anyang. The number of bronze drums is small. A bronze drum with a *Taotie* pattern of the late Shang Dynasty was unearthed in Chongyang, Hubei, and is 75.5cm high with a drumhead diameter of 39.2cm, completely modeled on the wooden drum with a leather drumhead. A similar work is in the Izumiya Museum of Japan. The craftsmen copied the detailed characteristics of the wooden drum subtly and correctly represented the leather layer nailed on the drum and three rows of round nails on the drum rim. The bronze drum in the Izumiya Museum collection even vividly recreates the texture of the boa skin.

Shang. Chongyang Bronze Drum 75.5cm high, drumhead diameter 38cm, and weighs 42.8kg. Unearthed from Chongyang, Hubei Province in 1977. Kept in Hubei Museum.

Bell

The bell is the most important bronze musical instrument.

It first emerged in the Western Zhou Dynasty and was created when bronze smelting and casting technology and music reached a certain level in the Western Zhou Dynasty. According to researchers, the look of the bell was evolved from *Nao* of the southern area. However these two musical instruments have different usages. *Nao* has a handle beneath the mouth and is played with face upward; on the contrary, a bell is hung on the bell shelf with its mouth beneath the handle and is played with a wood mallet.

Western Zhou. Jingshu Bell
37.5cm high. Unearthed from Zhangjiapo, Chang'an county, Shaanxi Province in 1984. Kept in the Archeology Research Institute of the Chinese Academy of Social Sciences.

Bells can be divided into *Yong* (Handled Bell) and *Niu* (button-shaped bell) according to the way they are hung. The main part of both bells is the same, but there is column-shaped handle on the top of the *Yong* bell, on which a square or half-ring shaped handle is designed for hanging the bell on the bell hook; the *Niu* bell has a bridge-shaped handle on the top and can be directly hung on the bell hook.

A *Yong* bell typically consists of three parts, namely the *Yong* (handle), *Zheng* (front of a bell body) and tambour from the top to the bottom. The upper part of the bell is collectively named *Zheng*. The central part that was normally carved with inscriptions and both sides *Mei* (*Ruding* pattern, dot-shaped pattern) and *Zhuan* (cloud pattern). The lower part of the bell is

Warring States Period. Zenghou Yi Chime
273cm high, rack 748cm long, and weighs 2,500kg. Excavated from the Zenghou Yi tomb, Suixian county, Hubei Province in 1978. Kept in Hubei Museum.

named "tambour," the part that generates sound by striking. The decoration of the bell body mainly located at the *Wu* (the plain surface of the upper part of the *Zheng*), *Zhuan* and tambour. The pattern decoration of the tambour is often the image of a creature of half-dragon and half-bird with a long nose, standing back-to-back.

A single bell hung for use is called *Tezhong*. Several bells of

different sizes hung in order and used in combination were called chime bells. The chime bells of the middle Western Zhou Dynasty normally consisted of three bells. But the number of chime bells became increasingly larger as time progressed. A bronze chime unearthed from the tombs of *Zenghou Yi* of the early Warring States Period is the largest ancient bronze chime known so far, representing the highest level of bronze musical instrument manufacturing.

The *Zenghou Yi* Chime consists of 65 bells, including 45 *Yong*,

19 *Niu* and a percussion instrument called *Bo*. These musical instruments were hung intact on the square-shaped bronze-wooden structured bell shelf in eight groups in three rows. Together with the chime two long wooden clubs painted with colored lacquer were used to strike the bells, and six T-shaped wood mallets used for ringing the bells were unearthed. The chimes weigh 2,567kg in total. The largest bell is 203.6kg while the smallest one is only 2.4kg. It takes five musicians to play the chimes, two standing on one side striking the big bells with the clubs, while three others stand on the other side with two mallets each to ring the bells of the middle and upper rows.

Testing shows the *Zenghou Yi* chime still keeps its original tone. It boasts beautiful timber, wide compass, rich tones and relatively precise temperament and can play music with harmony, polyphony and modulation.

Except the small *Niu* bells hung on the upper row of the bell shelf are simple without decoration, the rest of the bells were carefully and elaborately decorated with complex and beautiful relief dragon patterns and *Panhui* designs and some were embedded with copper adornments on the handle.

The inscription on the chime has a total of 2,828 Chinese characters. Apart from the inscription "*Zenghou Yi* Made and Held" on the face of the *Zheng*, the rest are about music, offering important information for studying ancient Chinese music. Gold wire gilding technique was applied to many inscriptions, adding an impression of resplendence and luxury to the chimes.

The chime shelf was designed with full consideration of performance using, the structure and aesthetic needs. The size, volume, proportion and color combination of the different parts were carefully designed, compatible with the *Zhongju* (bell pole) *Bronze Figure*, gecko hook, animal-shaped column, openwork carving pedals and *Panchi* (coiled dragon) crossbeam bronze sheath. The chimes represent changes in unity, meaning and variety.

Bo

The *Bo* emerged in the late Shang Dynasty and early Western Zhou Dynasty and became popular in the early Spring and Autumn Period with *Bo* set emerged.

The top of the *Bo* is in the shape of a bridge or crouching animal and the bottom is not in arc shape but straight. The *Bo* produces different tones from the bell and was often played together with the bell. Some *Bo* works were decorated with relief bird and tiger designs, looks that were exquisitely carved, such as the *Xiao*-head *Bo* in the Palace Museum and the Four-tiger *Bo* in the Shanghai Museum collection.

Warring States Period. Chuwang *Bo*
92.5cm high, and weighs 134.8kg.
Unearthed from the Zenghou Yi tomb,
Suixian county, Hubei Province in 1978.
Kept in Hubei Museum.

Bronze Weapons

"The most important affairs of a country lie in sacrificial rites and military affairs," said the famous work *Zuo Zhuan* (*Commentary of Zuo*) before the Qin Dynasty.

In Xia, Shang and Zhou dynasties, the turmoil of war continued for years and weapon manufacturing became an important sector in bronze casting. Weapons and armor accounted quite a large share of the bronze casting during that time. For example, the bronze weapons unearthed from the *Fuhao* tomb, Yinxu, Anyang, Henan accounted for about 30 percent of the total bronze ware unearthed, second only to the ritual ware.

Shang. Fuhao *Yue*
39.5cm long, blade width 37.3cm. Unearthed from the Fuhao tomb, Anyang Yinxu, Henan Province in 1976. Kept in the National Museum of China.

In the tombs of Shang and Zhou dynasties, the quantity and proportion of weapons unearthed were even larger.

There are many kinds of bronze weapons; some were used for cut and thrust and some for chariot or horse fighting. The bronze weapons can be divided into the following types according to their functions:

Grappling weapons: mainly including dagger-axes, spears, halberds, *Shu* (long pole), *Pi* (long lance), *Qi* (axe), *Yue* (battle-axe), sword, and so on.

Long shot weapons: mainly featuring *Zu* (arrowhead), crossbow, and so forth.

Armor: mostly shields and armor, and so on.

Spring and Autumn Period. Spear of Wu's King Fuchai
29.5cm long. Unearthed from Mashan, Jiangling, Hubei Province. Kept in Hubei Museum.

Emperor Qin Shihuang (ruled 246–209 BC) confiscated all bronze weapons to Xianyang after he conquered the six kingdoms and unified China in 221 BC and cast 12 bronze figures each weighing 170,000kg. Though a great number of bronze weapons were destroyed at that time, many were preserved in nobles' tombs and ancient war fields. Some extremely exquisite works were especially made for the king, marshals and important ministers.

For example, the bronze *Yue* symbolizes the military power of the ruler. The *Yue* is a kind of large axe with an arc-shaped blade, tied to the long handle with the *"Nei"* and *"Chuan*(hole)*"* at the rear. The large bronze *Yue* unearthed from the noble tombs of Anyang, Henan province, Taixi Village, Gaocheng, Hebei province and Subutun Village, Yidu, Shandong province, have decorations featuring a tiger savaging people, and carved *Taotie* patterns, thus showing the special status of the holders.

During the Spring and Autumn Period and the Warring States Period, warfare was more frequent and nobles did not stop taking over cities and seizing the territories of the others. As the weapon materials and casting techniques were directly connected to the rise and fall of a kingdom, all kingdoms attached great importance to bronze weapon manufacturing. Wu, Yue and Chu kingdoms were famous for the superior weapons and this led to the establishment of famous sword casting couple Gan Jiang and Mo Ye in the Wu Kingdom.

Some extant weapons of nobles and famous ministers of the Eastern Zhou Dynasty presented high aesthetic expression in addition to the function of actual fighting. The makers were especially sensitive to the detailed changes such as symmetry, arc and curvilinear of the weapon. Some weapons were embedded with gold wire inlaid inscriptions.

The Sword of Yue's King Gou Jian unearthed from Chu's tombs in Jiangling, Hubei, is 55.7cm long, longer than the bronze swords of the Western Zhou Dynasty, and a middle ridge on both sides, and a better blade for cuts and thrusts. When it was unearthed, the sword was still sharp as if it was new with pressed blades. The face and back of the sword sheath were embedded with blue glaze and kallaite and the sword handle was decorated with beautiful diamond-shaped designs. The bird *Zhuan* inscription is near the sword sheath and reads "Sword made by Yue's King Gou Jian for his personal use."

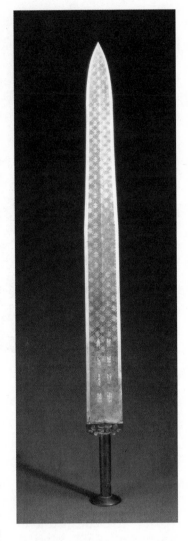

Spring and Autumn Period. Sword of Yue's King Goujian
55.7cm long. Unearthed from Wangshan, Jiangling, Hubei Province. Kept in Hubei Museum.
It has eight Chinese characters in the shape of a bird and worm Zhuan, recording Goujian, King of the Wu Kingdom, and the sword was made for his personal use.

Wu's King Zhiguang's Sword is similar to this one but shorter, and both sides of the sword handle were decorated with flame-shaped images.

The Spear of Wu's King Fu Chai was unearthed in Mashan, Jiangling, Hubei province, and was also decorated with diamond-shaped patterns, ridged along the central line, with a bloodlike groove. A relief of an animal face was cast at the end of the spear with the gold wire inlaid inscription, "Wu's King Fu Chai made for his personal use."

The weapons decorated with patterns of the same period include those from Sichuan. The patterns were not carved with machine and cannot be wiped out or grinded, reflecting advanced casting technologies of that time. According to a technical study from cultural relics circles, it was a special but exquisite surface alloy technology that features both decoration effect and anti-corrosion functions.

The famous weapons from the Spring and Autumn Period and the Warring States Period also included Song Gong *Ge*, Shaoyu Sword, Yan's King Xi's Spear, Caihou Chan's Sword, Chenhou Yinzi *Ge*, Shang Yang Halberd, Lu Buwei *Shaofu* (a department in charge of handicraft for the imperial family) *Ge*, Banian Lu Buwei *Ge*, Zenghou Yi Qin *Ge*, and so on.

The minorities such as the Donghu ethnic group in the north, Guyue ethnic group in the south and ethnic groups in Sichuan also created bronze weapons compatible with the local situation, habits of the ethnic groups and warring environments, creating distinctive ethnic characteristics.

Between the Gods and Man

An important part of bronze ware of the Shang and Zhou dynasties is the figure work with sculptural characteristics, and is mainly divided into the following categories:

First, containers or vessels in the shape of figure, for example *Hushiren You* (vessel in the shape of a tiger eating a man) of the Shang Dynasty and Changxin Palace Lantern of the Han Dynasty.

Secondly, independent figure sculptures, for example the bronze figure with religious meaning unearthed from Sanxingdui, Guanghan, Sichuan and *Jiyue Tongwu* (music performance house) of the Warring States Period unearthed from Shaoxing, Zhejiang;

Thirdly, stands in the shape of figures, for example the bell pole bronze figure that is large and figure-shaped ware legs and figure-shaped stands, which are small.

Figure-shaped Bronze Containers

The *Hushiren You* of the Shang Dynasty is also named *Ruhu* (tigerkin) *You*. There are two similar works collected in the world, one in France and the other in Japan. They are of a crouching tiger holding a person with its two front paws while the person crouches with both hands at the chest of the tiger and bare feet at the tiger's paws. Both the tiger and the person are decorated with *Kuilong*, snake and cloud and lightning patterns. The person's head is facing the tiger's wide open mouth but the person turns his head to the side as if nothing has happened. Some researchers believe art in the Shang Dynasty was not sophisticated enough to portray one's expression so that the person does not show

Shang. Hushiren *You*
32.5cm high. It is said the vessel was unearthed from Anhua, Hunan Province. Kept in the Musée Cernuschi, Paris.
The other *You* of the same shape and structure is in the collection of the Izumiya Museum of Japan.

any fear. Some researchers hypothesize that the work may be that the person was a deity engaging in sexual intercourse with the tiger. The person may perhaps be the ancestor of the Hu Kingdom of the Shang Dynasty. The five organs of the person in *Hushiren You* are quite precisely made. In order to measure the proportion between the person and the tiger holding each other together, the length of the lower limbs were shortened. The lower part of *You* and the tiger's two front paws and tail form three supporting points. The *You* has a hoop handle and a cap on which stands a small animal.

Among the figure works of the Warring States Period and the Western Han Dynasty, the most famous is the Changxin Palace Lantern unearthed from the Du Wan tomb in Mancheng, Hebei province. The inscription shows that the Changxin Palace Lantern was originally used in the Changxin Palace of the queen mother Du who was mother of Emperor Wudi (ruled 140–86 BC) of the Western Han Dynasty, and later was passed among several relatives of the imperial family. The gilded lantern was designed in the shape of a kneeling maid-in-waiting. The

Western Han. Changxin Palace Lantern
48cm high and weighs 15.78kg. Excavated from the tombs of the Western Han Dynasty in Mancheng, Hebei Province in 1968. Kept in Hebei Museum. On the body of the lantern are nine inscriptions, totaling 65 Chinese characters, recording the capacity, weight and travels of the lantern within members of the imperial family of the Western Han Dynasty.

Changxin Palace Lantern is a successful example of the systematic combination of dynamic figures and the application of structure and functions: the maid-in-waiting raises the lantern stand with her left hand and supports the chimney with her right hand, in the action of lighting for the others. In fact, the right arm is hollow and acts as the pipe discharging the smoke. The chimney, stand, the head of the maid-in-waiting and right arm can be dismantled for cleaning. The direction of the lamp and light intensity can be adjusted. The maid-in-waiting is beautiful, behaves in natural and graceful manners. It is also a vivid work as a sculpture.

Guanghan Bronze Figure Group

For a long time, knowledge about Chinese ancient sculpture was limited to the bronze ware in the shape of birds and animals and small-sized jade, stone and pottery sculpture works. An important fact unknown to the public was not unveiled until 1986, when a batch of bronze ware more than 3,000 years old was unearthed from two sacrificial pits in Guanghan Sanxingdui, Sichuan: Ancient China had cast figure sculptures in a large scale.

Most of the bronze ware unearthed from Sanxingdui was sacrificial rite

Shang. Bronze Standing Man
262cm high in total, the figure 172cm tall, and stands 80cm high. Unearthed from Guanghan Sanxingdui, Sichuan Province in 1986. Kept in Sanxingdui Museum.

Shang. Bronze head
Left: 36.7cm high. Right: 13.5cm high.
Excavated from Guanghan Sanxingdui, Sichuan Province in 1986. Kept in Sanxingdui Museum.

vessels. The most notable one is a standing bronze figure, which is 262cm tall in total, and the figure alone is 172cm, equal to the height of a person today. The figure looks lifelike and serious, wears lavish clothes and a hard cap with two interlaid O-shaped patterns on which there are flower-shaped decorations. The figure raises both his arms. The hands are large, making an empty ring with both Hukou (a part of the hand between the thumb and the index finger) facing each other. It is an action holding an item that has since been lost. Somebody reckoned it was a *Cong* (rectangular jade with round holes) for offering sacrifices to the god of the land, or a wand on behalf of the divine power or the emperor. The researchers believe the bronze figure might have been the head of soothsayers or a king of the ancient

Shang. Bronze mask
65cm high and 138cm wide. Unearthed from Guanghan Sanxingdui, Sichuan Province in 1986. Kept in Sanxingdui Museum

Shu kingdom.

The bronze figure has a square face, exaggerated five organs, thick and short eyebrows, almond-shaped eyes, sharp cheekbones that extend beyond the ears. His mouth is long. Both ears like fans with auricles in the cloud pattern shape. The earlobes have holes. By referring to the residues of the head portrait of the bronze figure unearthed at the same time, we can know the five organs of the bronze figure were colored: eyebrow and eye sockets in a reddish shade, eyeballs in black, mouth, and the nostril and ear holes in red. The demeanor is standard with the body straight, lacking vivid changes. However, the patterns, from the deformed dragon, interlaid O-shapes, triangles and panes on the clothes are refined and precise.

The 54 bronze heads unearthed together are about the same size as a real person's, some slightly smaller. Their faces can be divided into two types: one is similar with the bronze figure head, lifelike and solemn; the other is round with a garlic-shaped nose, without an obvious cheekbone line and the chin not in the

Shang. Head with gold mask
41cm high. Excavated from
Guanghan Sanxingdui, Sichuan
Province in 1986. Kept in
Sanxingdui Museum.

shape of wide ridge, but rounded naturally, looking gentle and kind.

The cap and hair style of the head portraits are different: some heads were designed in the shape to connect with a cap separately made; some wear an even-top cap; some wear horse tails; some wear twin-wing helmets and some have hair coiled on top of the head—which was common in rural areas of Sichuan. What is most unique is that some head portraits are covered with metal masks with eyebrow, eyes and mouth piercing. It may represent a special distinguished status. In ancient China, special materials such as gold and jade were connected with the most respected deities and they along with the Buddha were believed to have gold bodies.

The necks of the 54 bronze head portraits were made into bottom-up groove-shape and were used for inserting to the rest of the bodies. Thus it is believed the bronze head portrait is one part of the figure sculpture made of composite materials and the body must have been made from other materials.

The most mysterious is the bronze mask that looks like man, deity and animal simultaneously. The smallest one is only 6.5cm high, while the largest is 65cm high, with two extremely large ears that open like a halberd. The length between the two ears is 138cm. The most intriguing part is his eyeballs, which are in the shape of a long

Shang. Divine tree
390cm high. Unearthed from Guanghan Sanxingdui, Sichuan Province in 1986. Kept in Sanxingdui Museum.

Warring States Period. Jiyue Bronze Stand
17cm high, 13cm wide, and 11.5cm thick. Unearthed from Potang, Shaoxing, Zhejiang Province in 1981. Kept in Zhejiang Museum.

column, popping up 16.5cm above the eye sockets on both sides and the eyeball diameter is 13.5cm. The image with the pop-up eyeballs has never been seen in other areas before. Some believe the mask is the image of the ancestral deity of the ancient Shu kingdom—Can Cong in legend, according to the description about Shu's king Can Cong, "he has vertical eyes, and first named himself king," in *Huayang Kingdom Record* written by Chang Qu of the Jin Dynasty (265–420). There are square holes on the neck and earlobes on the mask, which must be especially made for inserting into the body made from other materials. The large size shows the mask will form a huge deity several times the size of a real person after connecting with the body made from other materials. Another piece is smaller than this one, but also with pop-up eyeballs. On the nose of the mask a 66-cm long three-dimensional decoration in the shape of a coiling cloud is embedded, rising high above the head, unique and strange.

If put together, the 50-odd head portraits and nearly 20 masks in different sizes referring to the standing bronze figure, there is a grand group of sculptures combining man and deity. The solemn and supernatural images will be enforced because of the collective powers they hold. The viewers will be shocked in the religious cold and killing environment.

There are six bronze divine trees that co-exist with the bronze portraits. The largest one is 3.9m high with branches hanging fruits and birds, and dragons flying across the branches. Two small bronze figures kneeling back to back are on the stands of the two trees. Some believe the divine trees are *Jianmu* or *Dishen* (god of the land), which are linked with heaven in ancient legends.

Sanxingdui bronze ware created in ancient Shu displays a highly developed culture center more than 3,000 years ago. The strange and unique shape is different from the bronze ware in the central plain that most people are familiar with. Thus some believed Sanxingdui Culture was from other country, or even from another planet. However, the bronze Zun and jade ware unearthed from the same place show the close relationship between Sanxingdui Culture and that of the central plain.

There is small bronze ware with sculptures meaning they were from the Shang and Zhou dynasties, for example, the *Jiyue Tongwu* of the Warring States Period unearthed from Potang, Shaoxing, Zhejiang. A group of naked bronze figures in the house are dancing and singing. Researchers believe it may represent religious activity of the ancient Yue people. The bronze house is 17cm high, and on the top there is an octagonal column with a large bird resting on top, or totem pole. Under the pole it is a roof with four edges curling towards the top. The house has three chambers, divided by two columns. Both walls have hollowed pane patterns and the back has a cross-shaped small window. There are six kneeling bronze figures in the house. In the front row, one is beating a drum and two females are singing. At the back row, three bronze figures are accompanying the singers with *Sheng* and *Qin* (musical instruments). The figures are small in size, but the five organs are vivid and the action and musical instruments are detailed, representing the living environment and customs of the ancient Yue people.

Figure-shaped Stands

There is a large number of bronze ware in great varieties with figures as the tool stand in ancient China. Since the Western Zhou Dynasty, for items in the shape of figurines, the figure is typically dressed in a cap and clothes, representing different status. For example, the figure-shaped linchpin unearthed from Beiyao, Luoyang, Henan, the bronze figure wears a net-shaped pin with a scarf tied beneath the chin, dressed in a long robe with a mandarin collar, which is long enough to cover his knees, and has a belt around the waist. The figure has both hands crossing his chest, and stands on his feet, representing a specific figure in reality. The figure-shaped legs supporting different vessels are normally in the image of naked men or women. For example, the square box shaped vessel unearthed from the Quwo, Shanxi, Jinhou tomb of the late Western Zhou Dynasty has four naked figures as its legs; all the figures support the vessel's bottom. From the

Western Zhou. Square Box-shaped Vessel 23.1cm high. Excavated from the Jinhou tomb, Quwo, Shanxi Province. It is now in the Shanxi Archeology Research Institute.

special hairstyles we can judge they are captives of other ethnic groups and were slaves.

There are some bronze works of the Western Zhou Dynasty representing slaves suffering from *Yuexing* (punishment of cutting off feet), reflecting cruel reality. *Yuexing* is a criminal law of ancient China, under which the punished have their feet

Western Zhou. Yuexing Slaver Doorkeeper *Ge*(part)
13.8cm high. Kept in the Palace Museum.

Warring States Period. Zhongju Bronze Figure
79cm-96cm high in total. Unearthed from the
Zenghou Yi tomb, Suixian, Hubei Province in 1978.
Kept in Hubei Museum.

cut off, belittled by the public and sent to act as doorkeepers
or defend a garden. The Yuexing Slaver Doorkeeper *Li* (food
container) kept in the Palace Museum consists of two parts: the
upper part is a container and the lower part is in the shape of a
house with a door that opens to the front wall. The rest of the
three walls have hollow windows. It can be used to fire and heat
food. The door can be opened or closed. On the left door, there
is cast a naked male doorkeeper, whose left foot was cut off, and
supports himself with a stick. A *Yueren* (a person suffered from
Yuexing) Doorkeeper Ding unearthed from Fufeng, Shaanxi, has
a complex structure. The doorkeeper was cast outside of the right
door, wearing a bob on his head, holding a door bolt in his chest,
naked, with his left foot cut off. A Yueren Guarding the Garden

Bronze Cart was unearthed from Wenxi, Shanxi. On the carriage, monkey and birds and crouching animals, which can rotate, were cast, simulating a garden with birds and animals inside. On one side of the carriage the door is open, with a naked person with the left foot cut off.

Among the large bronze works with figures with practical usage, the best representative is the six *Zhongju Bronze Figure* on *Zenghou Yi* chimes.

The *Zhongju Bronze Figure* is located on the middle and bottom rows of the chime, three to a row. The bronze figure is in the image of a warrior, standing at attention, wearing a round flat-headed cap, long gown with the right fabric covering the left, a belt, a long sword on the right, raising both arms to support the crossbeam. The maker properly adjusted the structure and length of the shoulder, elbow and forearm of the *Bronze Figure* according to the position and support function of different bronze figures.

The bronze figures on the lower row are larger than the middle row, about 1m tall, and good looking. The figures were colored and the gowns were decorated with red lines against the black background and petal patterns on the front of the garments. The middle row bronze figures have square tenons on the heads

Warring States Period. Bronze figure-shaped lamp (silver-headed bronze figure which holds a hornless dragon)
66.4cm high. Unearthed from Pingshan county, Hebei Province, tomb of the King of the Zhongshan Kingdom in 1977. Kept in Hebei Cultural Relics Research Institute.

Warring States Period. 15-Lamp Set
82.9cm high. Excavated from
Pingshan county, Hebei Province,
tomb of the King of the Zhongshan
Kingdom in 1977. Kept in Hebei
Cultural Relics Research Institute.

and feet to connect with the crossbeams. It is the first time images of strong and confident young warrior appeared in ancient artworks in China.

There are many vivid figures on the lamps of the Warring States Period and the Han Dynasty. The figure-shaped bronze lamp unearthed in Zhucheng, Shandong province, is a server who wears a broad belt, stands on a carved animal-shaped stand and holds a lamp in both hands. He slightly bends both knees with the lamps one higher and the other lower, reflecting the lamp holder cannot shoulder the burden well.

The bronze figure-shaped lamp (silver-headed bronze figure which holds a hornless dragon) unearthed from Pingshan, Hebei province, tomb of the King of Zhongshan Kingdom of the middle Warring States Period was cast with different materials. The main body is a man with silver head and bronze body standing on a square stand, who wears his hair coiled up. The eyeballs of the figure were made of black balls. The man dresses in a brocade gown with loose sleeves, painted with red cloud patterns, and wears a belt. He holds a hornless dragon in each hand to support three lamps, which have three candleholders. The hornless dragon is raised high on the right hand was cast with the decoration of the hornless dragon chasing a monkey.

A 15 bronze-lamp set unearthed from the Zhongshan Kingdom tomb consists of a lamp stand and seven sections of lamp racks. The central lamp standard is connected with seven arc-shaped branch racks, which holds a lamp calyx. In the center of the calyx is a candle holder. The lamp stand is round, decorated with three openwork-carving dragons. It has three double-body tigers, which hold a ring at their legs. Two figures on the standard, topless, are throwing food upwards. Echoing to the two people are monkeys playing on the lamp branches, some are climbing while others hang upside down to catch food. On the stand there are two big birds. On the top of the stand there is a dragon climbing upwards. With the activities of the persons, birds and animals on the bronze ware, the artisan represented a space connecting earth with heaven, full of vigor.

Moreover, it was popular to add decoration with figures or head portraits on bronze ware in the Shang and Zhou dynasties. The decorations have different meanings, and some of them may be the image of divine-man.

Beauty of Patterns: from Legend to Reality

The combination of color pattern decorations and unique molds creates unique charms of bronze ware of ancient China. The bronze pattern decorations can be dated back to the ceramic designs represented with color paintings and depicting the Neolithic Age. The bronze patterns mark the different changes in the progressing periods of bronze art development.

In the early days of the Shang and Western Zhou dynasties, bronze ware pattern decoration mostly involved animals in legends and images, strange with thick shades of religion. From the middle of the Zhou Dynasty, the decoration gradually evolved into simple and abstract patterns. In the Spring and Autumn Period and the Warring States Period, bronze-ware making turned towards color and gilding, splendid and luxurious beauty and the pattern decoration became refined and exquisite, even complex. At the same time, designs were themes of daily life activities such as banquets, entertainment, hunting and fighting, indicating bronze ware art in China was transforming from the image of the divine world to the real world of humans.

Li Zehou, a specialist in aesthetics, once described bronze ware art in the book *Course of Beauty* as "the beauty of ferociousness." He said, "If you look at the famous *Ding* of Shang and early Zhou dynasties, the battle-axe with an animal face, the lightning patterns decorated on bronze ware, the *Kuilong* and *Kuifeng* snarled with the *Taotie*, the deformed animals which did not exist in the real world, for example the mysterious night messenger – *Chixiao*, the horrible man-faced *Ding*…. They are no longer the vivid, lifelike images in Yangshao color ceramic patterns, nor the mysterious but abstract geometry patterns. They are deformed, stylized, horrible animal images. What they present are a mysterious power and the beauty of ferociousness."

The ferocious and mysterious patterns can be described as the

Liangzhu Culture
Liangzhu Culture is one of the relics of the Neolithic Culture in China, and it got its name because it was first discovered in Liangzhu town, Yuhang, Zhejiang province in 1936. It was mainly distributed in Taihu Lake area, the lower reaches of the Yangtze River, about 5,300 to 4,000 years ago. The most important discovery in the cultural relics was jade ware. Besides, the pottery unearthed was also delicate. There were also signs of written characters and city.

most attractive parts and attach strong emotional color to the bronze ware. However, the specific meaning of different patterns created in the remote ages is still a puzzle not completely solved.

Mysterious Patterns of Animals

Taotie Pattern

The *Taotie* pattern, the most popular bronze ware decorative design in the Shang and Zhou dynasties, was named by scholars of the Song Dynasty (960–1279) according to records in literature of the Warring States Period of *Master Lu's Spring and Autumn Annals*. According to *Master Lu's Spring and Autumn Annals*.

Taotie pattern in the early Shang Dynasty

Taotie pattern in the middle Shang Dynasty

Xianshi Review, Ding of the Zhou Dynasty was decorated with *Taotie*, which featured "only a head without a body." The *Taotie* pattern on the bronze ware was identical with the records. However, the *Taotie* design first appeared on *Ding* of the Shang Dynasty instead of Zhou Dynasty, several hundreds years earlier than that the record. In addition to the monster without a body in a *Taotie* image, some had a body, paw and tail. Therefore, somebody argued to rename it as "animal face pattern." However, most people like to use the mysterious name *Taotie* to name the design.

The typical *Taotie* pattern is a full-face round-eyed animal head, with sharp teeth and horns. Some *Taotie* images show a full-face head formed by two sidled *Kuilong* patterns. In all the *Taotie* patterns, the eyes are always the focus. The huge eyes leave an awesome impression on viewers even from a distance.

The *Taotie* pattern features rich variations from one bronze ware piece to another because one ceramic mold could only cast one bronze work in the early days of casting. The most obvious difference between *Taotie* patterns are the horns, some have ox horns, some sheep horns, and some have tiger's ears. People can distinguish the animal origin from the different images.

What does the *Taotie* design symbolize? Many believe it has religious meaning, aimed at making the bronze ware more solemn and applicable to religious occasions. Some scholars say the *Taotie* pattern represents the image of the god of heaven in ancient religions through textual research. It maybe a lasting riddle, as the real meaning of the mysterious design leaves a boundless imagination for people.

The *Taotie* design was normally applied on the main part of the bronze ware and formed a decorative face with the vertical *Kuilong* pattern or bird image together with the supporting patterns on both sides. The symmetrical design makes the *Taotie* pattern applicable to different parts of the ware, plain or curved surface, and does not produces deformations.

The *Taotie* patterns on the bronze ware in early days were formed with raised lines and were relatively simple. In the middle of the Shang Dynasty, the *Taotie* pattern evolved into an image formed with several layers of lines, named "Three-Layer Pattern," where the theme pattern is a relief image, on which different designs are carved; and under the theme pattern, refined and detailed cloud patterns are also carved.

The cloud pattern, or cloud and lightning pattern, are detailed spiral patterns. When weeding out the basic rendering, the clever ancient craftsmen created patterns on the rendering to set off the theme pattern. The "Three-Layer Pattern" technique produces multi-layered color expressions to the *Taotie* pattern and creates a stronger visual impact.

Taotie patterns were popular in the Shang, early Western Zhou and Eastern Zhou dynasties, but these designs lost the original "ferociousness".

The patterns of *Kuilong*, Panlong Dragon, Phoenix and Bird and Silkworm were also popular together with the *Taotie* pattern, in addition to the round eddy and four-petal flower patterns.

Dragon Pattern

The dragon is a fantastic animal in Chinese fables and legends, and was worshipped as the god of water by the ancient people.

In bronze designs, all the dragon images of snakes with horns are collectively named "dragon pattern." The most common one is the *Kuilong* pattern.

The *Kuilong* pattern typical refers to the side dragon design with a bow-shaped body, horns, huge eyes and bucked teeth, some with fin-shaped talons. It has changed many times and can be applied in various positions. It often appears with the *Taotie* pattern, sometimes clutching the horns of the *Taotie*, sometimes

Kuilong pattern

Coiled Dragon pattern

acting as the supporting image along the *Taotie* pattern to fill a blank space. It can also form a continuous decoration belt independently. The *Kuilong* pattern was often used alternating with the round eddy pattern to form two continuous designs, which are named *Huolong* (fire dragon) pattern.

The dragon pattern features many variations and are applicable to different decorative locations. It can be used as the theme pattern in a sequence or face-to-face to form a decoration belt, or appears on the curved surface of the mouth of *Zun* or *Gu* or belly of *Ding,* and so on as supporting patterns.

The dragon pattern is often decorated on the bronze plate

bottom in combination with images such as fish to form a vivid aquatic world.

There is also a snail-like dragon image on some ancient bronze ware, which has a long nose and coiled body. It is a unique and important pattern decoration of the Zhou clan.

Phoenix and Bird Patterns

The phoenix and bird pattern was common in the Shang and Zhou dynasties. The phoenix is an auspicious bird integrating characteristics of different birds and known as the king of birds. The phoenix and bird pattern was normally used on main decorative surfaces, on which the bird has a beautiful comb, some with horns, and long feathered tail. The bird pattern with a long tail and small-bird pattern were popular in the late Shang and Western Zhou dynasties and were often used on the decoration belt or as supporting patterns.

A special pattern is the *Chixiao* design. When it is the main

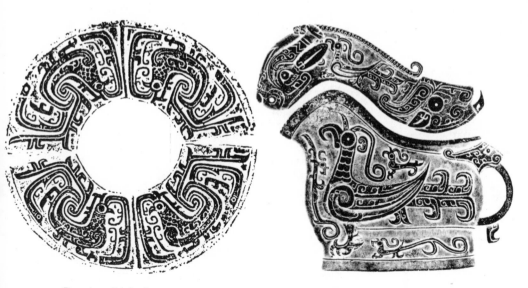

Phoenix and bird pattern

The application of the phoenix and bird . patterns (Shang. Miefu Yi *Gong*)

decoration, the *Chixiao* pattern is normally a full-face image. As *Xiao* and the like have faces, feathers, and horns, it can be easily distinguished from the others.

Abstract Patterns

Curled and Ripple Patterns

Since the middle of the Western Zhou Dynasty, some specific patterns gradually became abstract and formed a new design

Curled pattern

called curled pattern. It was given this name following the description of *Master Lu's Spring and Autumn Annals*: "*Ding* of the Zhou Dynasty has a curled pattern which is long and curves on both ends." The curled pattern basically consists of a horizontal S, meeting the characteristics of "curved on both ends."

It is obvious the curled pattern was developed from the bird and dragon patterns. If the bird patterns are arranged in parallel, we can assume the bird pattern evolved into the curled pattern.

Interlaid ring pattern

The curled pattern was widely used and varied according to requirements to decorate different part of different items.

.The interlaid ring and scale patterns were also popular during

Ripple

the same period of the curled pattern. The interlaid ring pattern often consisted of continuously distributed ovals and rings and was used to decorate the mouth and legs of the object. The scale pattern is like scales of aquatic animal, interlaid, and used to decorate a large area of the item.

The ripple (ring-shaped pattern) is a wide and smooth curled pattern, filled with shaped pattern in the trough of the continuous S-shaped patterns. It also features many changes. The ripple shows an obvious evolutionary relationship with the dragon and snake patterns.

Though abstract patterns were popular in the Western Zhou Dynasty and evolved from previous animal face, dragon and bird patterns, most of the mysterious meaning was lost, showing the general trend of art moving towards the rational in the Western Zhou Dynasty.

Panhui, Feather and Deformed Cloud Patterns

Since the Eastern Zhou Dynasty, bronze ware decorative design tended to be complex and refined with great varieties and endless changes. Generally speaking, they can be divided into two basic patterns: one is a lively one such as the *Panhui* pattern formed by coiled small snakes; the other is clear and neat and precise patterns formed by triangular cloud patterns. The former is mostly in shallow relief, while the latter is splendid and luxurious with gilding and colored paintings.

The *Panhui* pattern was created to meet new aesthetic needs. It was developed from a smaller and deformed *Kuilong* pattern. The simple pattern forms a large area decoration by repeatedly connecting the patterns to produce a gorgeous effect like brocade. The larger image of the same work was named the *Panchi* pattern.

These kinds of designs were made with the pressing die method, where four continuous pattern combinations were pressed on the object as it was being made. The pressing die method ensured that the pattern style and form on the object were consistent, and a die was used repeatedly for several items, saving time and manpower.

The feather, or wave pattern, was also popular during the same

Panhui pattern

Panchi pattern

time of the *Panhui* pattern. It was often applied on vessels such as *Bu* (vase) and *Lei* (drinking vessel) with a net-shaped design along its border. The relief pattern interval was very complex, looking like numerous fine feathers or roaring fine waves. But if examined carefully, viewers will find the head and talons of the dragon hiding in the pattern.

The deformed cloud pattern was normally in the frame of a triangle, circle or heart, embedded and inlaid with fine gold, sliver or rose copper wire, or embedded with kallaite. Some cloud patterns were in combination with floating and smooth cloud formations. This expressive method was passed on and used until the Han Dynasty.

Feather pattern

Lifelike Patterns

In the Shang Dynasty bronze ware decorative patterns, there were many lifelike animal images, for example birds, elephants, deer, rabbits and cicadas. But the craftsmen of that time often changed the look of the animal images in the process of creation and added many imaginary elements; for example, adding horns to the elephant to add some divine color to the object. In the Western Zhou Dynasty, the lifelike features of the animal designs greatly enhanced.

In the late Spring and Autumn Period and the early days of the Warring States Period, the decorative patterns of the bronze ware included some realistic images directly from daily life of that time, including banquets and entertainment, mulberry picking, archery, fighting, hunting, and so forth. The main expressive methods include depicting the image on the same layer as the background and adding another layer, embedding the image with metal of different colors and needle carving. The first two methods were often used for the kettle, mirror and *Dou* (standing cup). The kettle with images of banquets and entertainment, mulberry picking, fishing and fighting are collected by the Palace Museum and are the most famous representative work.

The bronze kettle, unearthed from Baihuatan, Chengdu, Sichuan, is 40cm tall with the diameter at the spout of 13.4cm.

(Warring States Period) Copy of scenes of a banquet, entertainment, hunting, fighting on sea and land, and defending (from a bronze kettle unearthed from Baihuatan, Chengdu).

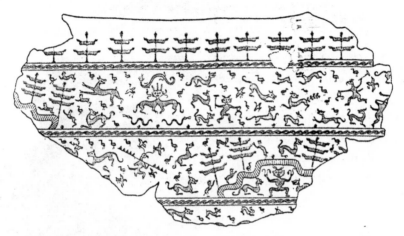

(Warring States Period) Copy of patterns and images (from bronze relics unearthed from Gaozhuang, Huaiyin, Jiangsu Province).

The kettle was decorated with four rows of decorative patterns from top to bottom. The image on the left side of the first row is that of an archery scene. A group of nobles are practicing archery. The image on the right illustrates several women on a tree picking mulberry leaves with somebody helping them from under the tree. On the second row on the left side is the image of a banquet and entertainment. The right side shows people kneeling on the ground shooting flying birds; in the third row there is an image of fighting. The image on the left is a scene of fighting and defending on land, while the one on the right is a scene of fighting at sea; the fourth row shows a hunting scene. The hunters are killing running animals with spears.

The figures, animals, trees and objects in the patterns are silhouettes, simple but vividly describing the activities. What's more, the method narrates the facts clearly and orderly. This expressive method directly evolved from the stone carving arts of the Han Dynasty.

Character Decoration

In the beginning, bronze ware inscriptions were in discreet places, such as the interior surface of vessels and on handles. Since the Eastern Zhou Dynasty, some bronze ware inscriptions were put in prominent places as decorations.

The earliest vessel is Luanshu Fou of the Jin Kingdom during the Spring and Autumn Period. The vessel is smooth and has no lines or decorations. The inscription, including 40 characters in four lines, is on the neck and shoulder of the object. Gracefully manipulated metal is decorated between the strokes. Typical similar objects include E Jun Qi *Jie* (*Jie* is an authorization for water and road transport issued by ancient emperors or courts).

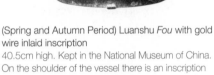

(Spring and Autumn Period) Luanshu *Fou* with gold wire inlaid inscription

40.5cm high. Kept in the National Museum of China. On the shoulder of the vessel there is an inscription of 40 Chinese characters in five lines, recording the merits Dafu of the Jin Kingdom Luanshu attacked the Zheng Kingdom and later defeated the Chu Kingdom.

The character structure of bronze ware inscriptions gradually evolved into patterns to satisfy decorative requirements. Metal-inlaid bird and insect patterns can be seen on the weapons used by nobles of the Wu, Yue, Chu, Cai and Song fief states during the Spring and Autumn Period. The styles lasted until the Han Dynasty. Inscriptions on some bronze vessels are like decorative designs, and it can be hard to distinguish inscriptions from patterns.

History Recorded in
Inscriptions

Bronze ware inscriptions are also called metal text. Most bronze ware inscriptions are found on bells and vessels, so the inscriptions are also called bell and vessel writings.

Bronze ware inscriptions consist of the artisan's name, production date, production purpose and related details. Inscriptions carry rich historical and cultural information and are significant archives. With bronze ware inscriptions, later generations have a chance to know the background to the making of the object, name individual object, judge production time, and carry out research.

The number of bronze vessels with inscriptions is more than 10,000. The first-hand material testifies, complements and corrects history books. Some important bronze ware inscriptions are important evidence for the Period Division Project of Xia, Shang and Zhou dynasties and research of ancient Chinese times.

Inscriptions in Shang and Zhou dynasties have the same structure with the inscriptions engraved on animal bones or tortoise shells during the same period. Both have the earliest systematic characters in China, and are also important sources of Chinese calligraphy. The strokes of the inscription chirography formed through writing, engraving and casting is substantial and symbolic. This is the powerful and implicative brushstroke effect that ancient calligraphers pursued.

Inscriptions in the Shang Dynasty

The number of inscribed characters on bronze ware of the Shang Dynasty is usually low, sometimes two or three. Some inscriptions are tribe marks created with figures and characters, some are names of the craftsmen, and some are posthumous titles of sacrificed ancestors. Despite of the limited number of characters, inscriptions and bronze ware in the Shang Dynasty represent flourishing mentality and confident creativity. Simuwu

Shang. Simuxin *Ding* inscription

Shang. Xiaochen Yu Rhinoceros *Zun* inscription
The inscription, totaling 27 Chinese characters in four lines, records that Xiaochen Yu (a noble in the late Shang Dynasty) followed the Emperor of the Shang Dynasty to attack the kingdom of Fan and was rewarded by the emperor and made the vessel to record the achievement.

Ding and Simuxin *Ding* of Fuhao tomb are typical. Each of them has inscribed three Chinese characters. The character layout seems grand. The character Si for Simuwu is at the top. Its strokes form a triangle, so the character has a structural center. Though the layout is not symmetrical, the characters convey a stable structure. The strokes are properly arranged and the spaces between strokes are appropriate in size. The character Mu for Simuxin is vertically extended and is put on the right side, responding to the other two characters. The last stroke of character Xin is very powerful. The strokes of the characters in both inscriptions are soft and hard, light and heavy, thin and thick.

In late Shang Dynasty, some inscriptions consisted of more characters, such as those on the Shusizi *Ding* and Xiaochenyuxi *Zun*. These inscriptions represent different calligraphic styles. The characters inscribed on the Shusizi *Ding* are straight in rows and columns, and one character decorates adjacent ones. The inscription on the vessel starts an official precise, orderly inscription style. The font of the inscription on the Xiaochenyuxi *Zun* is fat and consistent. The strokes change in size, weight and space.

Inscriptions in the Western Zhou Dynasty

The number of pieces of bronze ware with inscriptions in the Western Zhou Dynasty is high, and the number of inscribed characters is also high, and even reaches up to 500. At the same time, the content of the inscriptions is different from the past.

According to the Book of Rites that records and argues ritual procedures before the Qin Dynasty (221–206 BC), "Inscriptions are the words of achievements, merits and reputations of ancestors recorded on sacrificial articles to commemorate them." The most important purpose of the inscriptions is to eulogize the merits and virtues of ancestors. The first half of the inscription on the *Shiqiang Pan*, which was cast in the period of Emperor Gongwang of the Zhou Dynasty (922–899 BC), describes the stories of six emperors from Emperor Wenwang to Emperor Muwang, and the second half lists the merits made by five generations of the Wei family that assisted the six emperors.

Some inscriptions of bronze ware in the early period of the Western Zhou Dynasty record the activities that nobles took part in sacrificial ceremonies and expeditions and were awarded with shells, vehicles, horses, land and helpers. Nobles made bronze ware to record their merits, sacrifice to their ancestors, and show off their achievements to later generations. The format of most of these pieces of bronze ware with such kind of inscriptions was stable and steady, and the patterns were splendid. The inscription font is serious and strict, conveying a divine flavor. These feature sobriety of ritual articles.

In the middle and late period of the Western Zhou Dynasty, more and more bronze ware inscriptions recorded contracts. The inscriptions are equivalent to contracts between nobles.

Western Zhou. Yu *Ding* iscription
The inscription has 291 Chinese characters in 19 lines. The characters feature precise structure and vigorous style, and are representative works of the official chirography of the Western Zhou Dynasty.

The inscription on the Gebo *Gui* records the agreement that Gebo exchanged land with horses and demarcated the plot. The famous *Sanshi Pan* is named after the *Sanshi* characters in the inscription. Some people consider the artisan is Shi, so the article is also called *Shiren Pan*. The inscription has 357 characters, describing how the Shi people invaded the San state, and took over land from the San state. The inscription includes details of the positions of the land plots and demarcations, the personnel who participated in the demarcation and agreement on both sides, as well as the ministers in charge of the lawsuits of the imperial court of Zhou Dynasty.

The content of the bronze ware inscriptions in the Western Zhou Dynasty covered sacrifices, awards, expeditions, appointments of landlords, decrees of emperors, land transactions, and exchanges in population. The inscriptions

Western Zhou. Sanshi *Pan* inscription
Unearthed from Fengxiang, Shaanxi Province. Kept in the National Palace Museum in Taipei. The inscription has 349 Chinese characters in 19 lines. The chirography has profound influence on Chinese calligraphy since the end of Qing Dynasty.

provide a great deal of first-hand material for historical research of the Western Zhou Dynasty.

Some inscriptions describe key historical events and figures and have precious historical research value. The *Li Gui* was discovered in Lintong, Shaanxi, in 1976. On the eighth day after Emperor Wuwang of the Zhou Dynasty defeated Emperor Zhou of the Shang Dynasty, Li, a noble in the Zhou Dynasty, was awarded by Emperor Wuwang and cast a piece of bronze ware. According to the inscription and related documents, researchers conclude that the date when Zhou defeated Shang was January 20, 1046. The *Li Gui* became an important evidence for the Chronology Project of Xia, Shang and Zhou dynasties, and has the earliest inscribed age among all pieces of bronze ware with inscriptions in the Western Zhou Dynasty. *Tianwang Gui*, another important bronze ware of the same period, recorded an event that Emperor Wuwang held a great appointment ceremony and made sacrifices to Emperor Shangdi of the Yin Dynasty and Emperor Wenwang of the Zhou Dynasty. The sacrifice changed the traditional priority of Yin emperors making sacrifices for Emperor Yin of the Yin Dynasty. The inscription on the *He Zun*, cast during the reign of Emperor Chengwang of the Zhou Dynasty (1042–1020 BC), recorded the historical event that Emperor Chengwang moved to Chengzhou (Luoyi). *Lai Pan*, a piece of bronze ware unearthed in Baoji, Shaanxi, in 2003, has 372 characters inscribed on it, which record the merits of eight generations of the Shan family who assisted 12 emperors in the Western Zhou Dynasty (from emperors Wenwang to Xuanwang). The inscription verifies the titles of emperors of the Western Zhou recorded in *Zhou's Biography of Records of the Grand Historian* for the first time, and is valuable in studying the history of the Western Zhou Dynasty.

Bronze ware inscriptions of the Western Zhou Dynasty have

various styles of calligraphy, which can be divided into two types. One is the official orthodox elegant style, which stresses brush strength and grand vigor, such as the inscription on the *Dayu Ding*. The other is the freestyle way, which stresses calligraphic connotation and interest. Both styles have deep-seated influences on later painting and calligraphy art.

Inscriptions on large-size pieces of bronze ware, which were produced by workshops under the imperial court of the Zhou Dynasty and local kingdoms, have the same calligraphic style with the dimensions and decorative patterns of bronze ware. Both the calligraphy and decoration convey a strict and superb flavor. The inscription on the *Dayu Ding*, a representative piece, has 291 characters in 19 rows, and records the appointment of Yu, a noble in the 23rd year of the reign of Emperor Kangwang of the Western Zhou (997 BC). The font is dignified and square and has curved transitional strokes. The distances between the lines are equal, indicating considerable and strong vigor. The inscription on the *Qiang Pan*, a later piece of bronze ware after the *Dayu Ding*, has 284 characters in 18 lines, and the layout stresses the equal space between lines and columns. The character shape is more elegant and graceful, and strokes are subtle and shapely. The characters' shapes become longer. This represents a new trend of bronze ware inscription calligraphy after the middle of the Western Zhou Dynasty. Many long bronze ware inscriptions in the late period of the Western Zhou Dynasty emphasize a clean layout of lines. Some inscriptions even have character grids (such as *Dake Ding* and *Song* Kettle). Other inscriptions pay extreme attention to horizontal and vertical orderliness. As a result, the general layout seems loose.

Sanshi Pan (*Shiren Pan*) was made during the reign of Emperor Liwang of the Western Zhou Dynasty (877–841 BC, late period of the dynasty). The characters inscribed are square and short. Strokes from the left to the right are not horizontal and strokes from up to down are not vertical, but the characters' center are stable. The aesthetic features of vastness and generosity make the piece stand out among bronze ware inscriptions of the Shang and Zhou dynasties.

Other important bronze ware inscriptions of the Western Zhou Dynasty are characters on the *Maogong Ding*, *Guojizibai Pan* and *Zongzhou* Bell. There are 497 characters inscribed on the *Maogong Ding*, the longest one existing among Western Zhou inscriptions. The inscription on the *Zongzhou* Bell has 122 characters, and is the longest one among all bell inscriptions during the Shang and Zhou dynasties. The inscription on the *Guojizibai Pan* has a free and easy style of calligraphy, and is written in poetic form, which is rare in inscriptions. The inscription records that the noble Guojizibai conquered Xianyun, a minor tribe, under the order of the Zhou Emperor and was rewarded for fulfilling his duty.

Graphic Characters in Inscriptions of the Shang and Zhou Dynasties

Inscriptions of the Shang and Zhou dynasties have graphic characters like badges. Some researchers consider these graphic characters as tribe badges. On some bronze articles, the name of the one who is sacrificed is under the graphic character, or a frame is added to the graphic character, similar to today's seals.

The graphic character belongs to pictographs or associative compounds in philology. Due to the specifics of graphic characters, people today are able to directly tell the meaning of the characters. This kind of graphic character leads to the belief that "calligraphy and painting have the same origins."

Graphic characters focus on the image of human beings and the relations between people.

Graphic character	Source	Connotation
	(Shang) Fu *Gong*	A woman works with a broom in her hand.
	Bronze ware group unearthed from Fuhao tomb of the Shang Dynasty	The character structure and font direction represent a mother taking care of her child.
	(Shang) Xiang *Ding*	Feast for exchanges
	(Shang) Xiang *Qi*	
	(Shang) Yayufuji *Gui*	Two people walk hand-in-hand.
	(Shang) *Ding*	A man stands on a boat carrying burdens on his shoulders.
	(Western Zhou) *You*	A man stands facing forward with shells (currency) on his shoulders.
	(Shang) Bufugui *Ding*	A man walks with footprints left behind.
	(Western Zhou) Lufuyi *You*	Soldiers gather under the flag, which has a flying band

Graphic characters also have distinct animal signs:

Graphic character	Source	Symbol
	(Western Zhou) Tiger *Gui*	Tiger
	(Shang) Gengshimafuyi *Gui*	Horses and pigs
	(Shang) Yamofuding *Zun*	A tapir walks on the grass.
	(Shang) Muyi *Zhi*	Three birds perch on a tree, looking around.
	(Shang) Ziyu *Zun*	A school of fish swim in the water.

The tribe, group and age of the bronze ware distributed in overseas countries can be determined in accordance with similar graphic characters.

Bronze Ware Inscriptions in the Eastern Zhou Dynasty

During the Spring and Autumn Period and the Warring States Period, Chinese calligraphy developed in diverse directions. Calligraphic relics consist of written characters, such as bamboo documents, alignment agreements, wooden figures, painted carpentry and textiles, and

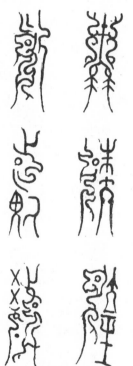

inscriptions on bronze ware, stone drums and seals.

As the imperial Zhou court rule declined, characters of other countries that were quite different from the ones of the Zhou Dynasty gained prominence. Two dominant systems came into existence during the Warring States Period. One was the western character system with the Qin Kingdom as a representative, and the other was the oriental character system with the six kingdoms to the east of Shanhaiguan Gate as their representatives. This oriental character system is called "ancient characters" by later generations. Qi and Lu Kingdoms and Chu, Xu, Wu and Yue Kingdoms in the southern part had typical characters.

Spring and Autumn Period. Caihou Chan Sword inscription
Unearthed from Huainan city, Anhui Province. The sword has an inscription of six Chinese characters in two lines. It is in the Anhui Museum.

Warring States Period. Inscription of the *Ding* of Zhongshan's King Guo (part)
Excavated from the tombs of the King of the Zhongshan Kingdom, Pingshan county, Hebei Province in 1978. Kept in the Hebei Cultural Relics Administration.
It has an inscription of 469 Chinese characters in 77 lines, all carved on the outer surface of the vessel.

Bronze ware inscriptions of the Eastern Zhou Dynasty had two artistic tendencies. One carried the rules from the Western Zhou Dynasty and paid much more attention to stroke and structure. Some inscribed characters were prudent, and others disregarded restrictions. Some special inscriptions were made with models, such as the inscription on the Qingong *Gui* of Qin Kingdom.

Another trend of inscriptions was an emphasis on decoration. Characters on bronze ware inscriptions unearthed from the Caihou tomb extended vertically, the strokes were rigid linear lines and arcs, and the structure seemed like patterns. This style can be obviously found in the bronze ware inscriptions unearthed from the Zenghouyi tomb. Only carving traces between the strokes can be seen, while the enthusiasm of writing and passion disappear. Bronze ware inscriptions of the Chu Kingdom have different styles. Some are free and unlimited, such as the characters on the *Gui* of the Chu's King Yanken. Some inscriptions intentionally pursue changes and novelty and modify strokes into decorative patterns. On the inscription of the *Pan* of the Chu's King Yanken, the beginning strokes are thin, transitional points are fat, and the ending strokes are in water drop shape. This calligraphic style is called "tadpole font" by later generations. In the Chu, Wu and Yue kingdoms, a bird font style was popular. Character structure and some strokes looked similar to bird shapes.

Among the large amounts of bronze ware unearthed from No. 1 tomb of the Zhongshan Kingdom during the Warring States Period in Pingshan County, Hebei Province, 90 pieces have inscriptions. The inscription of the Kettle of the Zhongshan's King Cuo has 448 characters, and 469 on the *Ding* of the Zhongshan's King Cuo. The inscriptions are detailed records of the lineage and big events of the Zhongshan Kingdom. The font is thin and tall, and beginning and ending strokes have sharp edges. The bird font features can be seen in some parts of font structure.

These inscriptions show that people in the Eastern Zhou Dynasty, in particular during the Warring States Period, intentionally pursued decorative aesthetics in calligraphy. However, this font style lacks writers' passion due to excessive emphasis on novelty. Therefore, the font style is mostly ignored in calligraphic history.

Western Han. Bronze Kettle with Bird Zhuan 44.2cm high. Unearthed from the tomb of the King Jingwang of the Zhongshan Kingdom, Mancheng, Hebei Province. Kept in the Archeology Research Institute of the Chinese Academy of Social Sciences. A beautiful bird Zhuan inscription and animal pattern belt were inlaid with gold and silver wire on the body of the kettle.

Convergence and Pluralism

China is a country of multiple nations. Different nations in different areas have their own characteristic cultures. After the Central Plains area stepped into the Bronze Age, surrounding areas experienced the emergence, development and flourishing of the bronze culture and created numerous pieces of bronze work with local features. Apart from the Sanxingdui bronze culture invented by ancient people living in today's Sichuan Province, ancient Dian and northern grassland bronze cultures are also remarkable.

Bronze cultures of neighboring nations have their own distinctive spiritual connotations and artistic styles, and at the same time are closely related to the bronze culture of the Central Plains. This exemplifies the convergence and pluralism feature of ancient Chinese bronze culture.

Bronze Ware of Ancient Dian People

Yunnan is in the southwestern frontier of China, and is the origin of Yuanmou man, the earliest mankind in China. Yunnan is also a main copper producing area. The region entered the Bronze Age in the 12th century BC and after hundreds of years of development, the bronze culture in Yunnan stepped into the flourishing period in the 4th century BC, when the Central Plains area was between the Warring States Period and the middle of the Western Han Dynasty.

Large-scale archeological and excavation activities aimed at the bronze culture in Yunnan started in the 1950s. In ancient tombs in Shizhai Mountain in Jinning, Lijia Mountain in Jiangchuan, and western part of Yunnan, more than 10,000 pieces of bronze ware, which were created by ancient Dian people, were dug up out of land, together with gold, jade and iron articles, and in particular, the snake-seated gold "Seal of the King of Dian."

Bronze ware of the ancient Dian people directly and broadly

reflected social lives, including sacrifices, wars, production and folk customs. These records of daily life can been found on bronze ware of shell containers, buttons, bottle gourd covers, pillows, needle and thread boxes, and weapons. Ancient Dian people used high-level production methods, and were able to cast articles with the lost wax process to represent scenes with complicated structures and many characters. In addition, gilt, tinning and jade inlay methods were adopted on bronze ware.

Shell containers, uniquely found among the ancient Dian people, were used to store seashells. Most covers on excavated shell containers are decorated with sculptures, which reflect complex events, such as war, sacrifice, sowing seeds and

Western Han. Shell container with sacrificial scene
53cm high and a diameter of 32cm. Unearthed from Shizhai Mountain, Jinning, Yunnan Province in 1956. Kept in the National Museum of China.

weaving. There are many objects and figures on the covers, but the layout is tidy and orderly. Most of figures featured are women, who are higher and bigger than adjacent people. Some women figures are gilt. This indicates traces of matriarchy prevailed in the ancient Dian society.

A shell container carved with a sacrificial occasion has the highest number of figures. The 32-cm-diameter cover is cast with 127 figures. A fence-style house and two large drums are centered on the lid. In the scene, the main woman, in splendid clothes and bare feet, sits on a tall bench on the platform under the roof. Other people hold drinking vessels and sit in front of the woman. Sixteen bronze also surround the woman. On the platform, a sacrificial animal is being killed. At the back of the main sacrificial woman are a pillar and a signboard. The pillar

Western Han. Shell container with battle scene
The cover diameter is 30cm. Unearthed from Shizhai Mountain, Jinning, Yunnan Province in 1956. Kept in Yunnan Museum.
The object's body was destroyed and only one cover remained, on which 13 figures were cast.

Western Han. Shell container with the scene of paying tributes
39.5cm high. Unearthed fromin Shizhai Mountain, Jinning, Yunnan Province in 1956. Kept in the National Museum of China.

shows the image of a snake swallowing a man, and a naked man to be punished is bound to the signboard. People in front of the naked man are beating the hanging bronze drums and *Chunyu*. A large kettle is placed outside the house, and bulls, goats, horses, pigs and tigers are tied up. Some have been killed, and others are being fed. On the edge of the lid are people riding horses, carrying items or doing other things.

Similar scenes include killing people and sacrificial bronze drums and pillars. The main sacrificial person is a woman on a palanquin. People who are to be killed for sacrifices are bound to signboards. Some people's feet are locked up, and some people kneel down with their hands tied behind their backs. Though the size of the people is small, the details and actions are specific.

Some bronze shell containers depict hand-to-hand combat.

Some commanders on horses hang the enemies' heads under the horses, and some enemies are trampled. A close battle between infantry is more cut-throat.

Different from the scenes of sacrifices and battles, those of sowing seeds, weaving and accepting tributes reflect more peaceful atmospheres. On the lid of a bronze shell container representing a scene of receiving tributes, there are people in different ethnic costumes. They lead bulls and horses that carry tributes on their backs. Some people are old, and some are women and children. Some people are looking beyond, as if they are carefully walking on the path just beside the cliff.

More bronze ware of ancient Dian people are decorated with zebus, which were the main livestock variety for the ancient Dian people. Horned zebus are portrayed on the tops of bronze bottle gourd covers, *Zun* and pots, and look as if they are standing on a mountain peak. When zebu herds are decorated on shell containers and thread boxes, a big zebu is in the center,

Warring States Period. Tiger Zebu Sacrificial Bronze
43cm high and 76cm long. Unearthed from Lijiashan, Jiangchuan, Yunnan Province in 1972. Kept in Yunnan Museum.

Warring States Period. Five-zebu Thread Box
31.2cm high, cover diameter 18cm. Unearthed in Lijia Mountain, Jiangchuan, Yuannan in 1972. Kept in Yunnan Museum.

Western Han. Three Tigers Biting Zebu Button
9cm high and 13cm wide. Unearthed from Shizhai Mountain, Jinning, Yunnan Province in 1956. Kept in Yunnan Museum.

surrounded by little zebus in the same direction and are lined up with equal intervals. It seems that the zebus are anxiously running forward.

On some bronze ware, some animals are depicted as harmonious and friendly creatures. On the cover of a shell container from the Warring States Period are a big zebu, three little deer and a small tiger. The zebu is licking the back of the tiger. Other images on bronze ware display animals fighting each other.

The Tiger Zebu Sacrificial Bronze is a masterpiece among bronze ware of the ancient Dian people. The principal part of the bronze is a simple, large zebu. The broad back is extended to a chopping board. The belly is hollow. The front and back legs are connected through the board's surface and the beams are at the hooves. A small zebu comes out from the square hole. A fierce tiger is biting the zebu's tail, and is climbing up with its back, with its claws digging into the zebu's legs. However, the zebu remains

Western Han. Bullfight Bronze Button
9.5cm long and 5.5cm wide. Unearthed from Shizhai Mountain, Jinning, Yunnan Province in 1956. Kept in Yunnan Museum.

upright. The artwork gives a sense of heavy and solid strength. The combination of a big zebu, a small zebu and a tiger brings complex special changes, and the structures are consistent. The surface is made up of the head, shoulders and back of the zebu creating a grand effect, and determines the artistic effect of the piece.

There are also some decorative buttons based on such social activities as sacrifices, fighting and dancing, as well as battles among animals. The subject matter and decorative methods on relief buttons of the ancient Dian People are similar to the decorative plates that were popular among nomadic groups on the northern grasslands.

Some buttons present scenes of society. For instance, there are scenes of killing people and zebus for sacrifices, soldiers' holding enemies' heads and escorting captured women and children, zebus and goats, and hunting tiger, deer and wild boars. All the events depicted are vivid and in detail. Some buttons present scenes of tigers, leopards and wolves hunting for herbivores.

Some scenes depict a few wild beasts hunting together, and some of wolves and leopards fighting each other for prey. At the same time, there are captured animals struggling and trying to escape. Typical buttons include the Two Tigers Swallowing Boar button and the Three Tigers Biting Zebu button. On the latter, a large tiger carries the killed zebu on its back, and two tiger cubs play beside the big tiger. The bronze represents cruelty of tigers and the animals' love for their children.

Western Han. Two-person Dancing Gilded Button
12cm high and 18.5cm wide. Unearthed from Shizhai Mountain, Jinning, Yunnan Province in 1956. Kept in Yunnan Museum.

Lively manners and gestures depicted on bronze ware indicate the ancient Dian craftsmen have carefully observed daily life and these events are reflected through extraordinary techniques of grasping the appearance and actions of creatures in the production process.

The Bullfight Bronze button unearthed in Shizhai Mountain shows the moment just before a bullfight performance. Spectators sit in the stands. A man in the middle bends down and opens the fence to free the zebus. On some pieces of work with similar scenes, some people sit beside the fence gate, with pheasant feathers on their heads. They may perhaps be necromancers or performers. Some buttons show happy occasions, such as two and eight people dancing. The Eight-person Dancing button, discovered in Shizhai Mountain, has two layers that depict performers on the stage and the accompanying band in the orchestra pit. The whole button is gilt, so the happy atmosphere

Western Han. Male Statue holding Umbrella
50cm high. Unearthed from Shizhai Mountain, Jinning, Yunnan Province in 1956. Kept in the Yunnan Museum.

becomes more intense. Winding long snakes are on the lower edges of most bronze buttons.

Bronze weapons and tools of the ancient Dian people were often added to many lively three-dimensional decorations. The scene of fighting between a tiger and a bear, and that of dogs capturing fish is illustrated on the tip of a spear. The scene of birds trampling snakes is shown on the edge of an axe. Ospreys and three men herding zebus can be seen on the tip of an arrow. Monkeys or foxes can be found on the edge of a battle-axe, while peacocks and rabbits are cast on sticks. Some bronze sculptures reflect daily life and customs at that time. On the handle of the Lietouwen Sword discovered on Lijia Mountain, a necromancer is holding a sword and a man's head. On the Xuanfu Spear unearthed on Shizhai Mountain, two naked slaves with their hands tied behind their backs are cast on both sides of the edge.

There are larger, individual bronze statues of men and women holding umbrellas. In general the statues are 40-50cm high. The figures wear splendid clothes and many accessories. They don't wear shoes, but kneel down or squat, and hold the umbrella handle with both hands. The facial features and figure proportions are precise and present respectful and restrained expressions.

Bronze ware of the ancient Dian people represents the true, specific daily life at that time in many aspects, including the oppression of the upper classes to lower classes, bloody battles, pleasure in life and fantastic imagination. The bronze ware has particular value in ancient art history and precious cultural values.

Bronze Ware of Nomads Living in the Northern Grasslands

In the northern grasslands from the northeast to northwest, the Donghu, Huns, Wuhuan and Xianbei nomads created unique cultures and arts.

According to archeological material discovered in modern times, the bronze culture created by the northern nomads started in the 13th century BC, around the late period of the Shang Dynasty in the Central Plains. Northern nomad bronze culture developed in the Western Zhou Dynasty, the Spring and Autumn Period, the Warring States Period, Qin and Han dynasties, and collapsed in the second century. The cultural climax was between the 4th century BC and the 1st century BC. The bronze ware of the grassland nomads is simple and clear, quite different from the deep and elaborate artistic styles of the bronze ware of the Central Plains.

Among the extant grassland bronze ware, decorative plates are the highest in number. Various plates decorated on belts, garments and harnesses were discovered in Liaoning, Inner Mongolia, Hebei, Shanxi, Shaanxi, Ningxia, Mongolia, the middle reaches of the Yenisei, and southern Siberia. Most bronze ware pieces were unearthed in Erdos, Inner Mongolia, so the nomads' bronze ware is also called Erdos bronze ware, known as Xifanpian.

Decorative plates of the Donghu people in the early ages were found in Inner Mongolia and Liaoning, and the designs are simple. From the Warring States Period to the Western Han Dynasty, the subject matter of the Huns' decorative plates are lively, and full of reliefs in animal shapes depicted on weapons, pole tips and harnesses which were popular.

Warring States Period. Bronze Deer Lying Down
Left: 11.5cm high, 15cm long. Right: 7.6cm high, 15.5cm long.
Excavated from Jungar banner, Ih Ju League, Inner Mongolia. Kept in the Inner Mongolia Museum.

Western Han. Plate of Two Horse Riders Hunting with Swords and Eagles on their Arms 11.1cm long, 8.4cm wide. Unearthed from Xichagou, Xifeng county, Liaoning Province in 1956. Kept in the National Museum of China.

Animal images were illustrated on most bronze plates, and some reflected folk customs. On some plates, pairs of animals, including bulls, horses, goats and camels, are enclosed in a rectangle with frames. Sometimes a single animal is enclosed in an oval without frames. Other plates display fierce fights between animals. The subject matter of decorative plates of the northern nomads is similar to that of the button decorations of the ancient Dian people, but the styles are different. The artistic style of the decorative plates from the northern grassland is stable and massive, such as the Two Bulls Plate unearthed in Xichagou, Xifeng, Liaoning. On the plate, two bulls bow their heads eating grass. The composition of the picture is sufficient, and the image is calm and powerful. The bulls are trained, domesticated and meek. Normally, images of fighting animals show a scene when the battle is over, with the weaker side succumbing to the loss, and the winner triumphing with the prey in its mouth.

In terms of production, both relief and line carving are used on decorative bronze plates of the northern nomads, and the charcoal was used to sketch object frames. Water drop-shaped ornamental signs outlined with charcoal can be seen in many pieces. This might be because of the processing of embedding kallaite on the bronze.

Typical decorative plates that reflect daily life include the plate of two horse riders hunting with swords and eagles on their arms, and the plate of knights capturing enemies. Both plates are discovered in Xichagou, Xifeng, Liaoning Province. A pair of decorative plates, found in No. 140 tomb in Kesheng Village, Chang'an, Shaanxi, show strong men getting off their horses, taking off their upper outer garments and wrestling. These plates represent the lively and unique customs of nomads living on the grassland.

Brilliant Sunset Glow

In 221 BC, the Qin Kingdom wiped out the other six kingdoms and established the Qin Empire, the first unified centralized country in Chinese history. Emperor Shihuang of the Qin Dynasty ordered all collected bronze weapons in the country to be sent to Xianyang shortly after the establishment of the country, and turned the bronze weapons into 12 huge bronze statues. This event marked the end of the Chinese Bronze Age.

The time of the Qin, Western Han and Eastern Han dynasties totals 441 years. The period was the beginning of Chinese feudalism and the ending of Chinese ancient bronze art.

In the new age, the bronze art was not as glorious as before and lost its dominant status. In the metal manufacturing industry, the emerging iron smelting technology became more prominent. The scope of the application of bronze ware reduced, and bronze ware was gradually replaced by gold and silver ware, porcelain and lacquer work. Bronze ware became a staple item. At that time, bronze ware mainly included lamps, smoking stoves, mirrors and harnesses. These practical articles carried the tradition during the Warring States Period in style, decoration and production, and became lighter and easier to carry. The bronze ware during the period was in two artistic styles. One was gorgeous and splendid, and the other was simple and elegant.

During the last development period of bronze ware, a large quantity of bronze articles were made in the Qin and Han dynasties. Bronze sculptures were especially brought to another level. In the history of Chinese sculpture, bronze sculptures before the Qin Dynasty were mainly small-sized decorations. In addition to Sanxingdui, other places had few large-sized individual full relief objects. During the Qin and Han dynasties, there were a lot of large-sized individual full relief articles. The sculptures were simple and smooth, and the style was unpretentious, grand and dramatic. Many bronze articles are representative works of Chinese sculpture.

Colored Painting Bronze Chariots and Horses in the Tomb of Emperor Shihuang of the Qin Dynasty

Terracotta warriors in the tomb of Emperor Shihuang of the Qin Dynasty were discovered in Lintong County, Shaanxi, in 1974, including an underground army made up of 8,000 terracotta warriors. At the end of 1980, two sets of painted bronze chariots and horses, half the size of real ones, were unearthed seven meters underground to the west of the tomb. The archeological discovery brought people directly acquainted to the large-sized bronze ware of the Qin Dynasty for the first time.

When the two-wheel bronze chariots pulled by four horses and

Qin. No.1 Bronze Chariot and Horse Painted with Color
225cm long. Excavated from the tomb of Emperor Shihuang of the Qin Dynasty in 1980.
Kept in the Museum of Qinshihuang Terracotta Warriors and Horses.

Qin. No.2 Bronze Chariot and Horse painted with Color
317cm long. Excavated from the tomb of Emperor Shihuang of the Qin Dynasty in 1980.
Kept in the Museum of Qinshihuang Terracotta Warriors and Horses.

a single shaft were unearthed, one was in front of another. High-level officials are driving the chariots, and the principal seats are empty. The large umbrella covers are thin, curved castings. An official driver stands in front of the chariot, while bows, arrows and shields are inside the chariot. This chariot is the leading one, and is also named an erected chariot, tall or *Rong* chariot. The back one is called *An* or *Wenliang* chariot. When Emperor Shihuang traveled through the country, he rode in this kind of chariot. The two chariots have more than 7,000 components and accessories, and 3,010 pieces were unearthed. It took archeologists eight years to recover them.

The two painted bronze chariots reflect the chariot system of the Qin Dynasty and embody supreme imperial powers. The smelting, casting, mechanical processing and painting technologies used on the chariots were incomparable at that time.

The No. 2 Bronze chariot (*An* chariot) is 328.4cm long, weighs

1,241kg, and is made up of 3,462 gold, silver and bronze parts and accessories. The bronze chariot, horses and the official driver are lively with colors painted on them. The color of white prevails, and vermilion, pink, purple, blue, green, black and brown patterns give out shinning and magnificent effect. The driver sits in the front chamber, and wears a hat, gown, waistband and sword. The official's face is pink, and the beard and eyebrows are engraved. The horses' bodies are pure white, and their tongues and nostrils are vermilion. Gray lines can be seen on horses' backs. The chariot is equipped with complete harnesses. The halters and chaplets are made of gold and silver. The light blue chains around the necks are made of very thin brass wires. The heads of the outside horses turn slightly outward, producing the vivid effect in an orderly team. A small banner is erected on the head of the rightmost horse. There are painted boards in colors in the front chamber of the chariot. Windows on the left and right walls of the back chamber are engraved with flowers. Cloud patterns were painted on the interior oval chariot cover, and a silk cloth covers the chariot's roof. It's surprising to see the complicated structure and sophisticated casting.

Bronze Horses of the Han Dynasty

It was popular to use bronze sculptures to decorate palaces and imperial gardens in the Han Dynasty. According to historical documents, bronze dragons and phoenixes were used as decorations on gates and palace roofs at that time. In the Western Han Dynasty, a bronze dragon was placed on the gate of Chang'an City, a bronze phoenix of 16m high was on the front gate of Jianzhang Palace, and bronze phoenixes were also on other buildings in Jianzhang Palace. Palaces in the Han Dynasty were ruined long before, and so people today have no chance to appreciate them. We can only imagine the grand, mythological

Western Han. Gilded Bronze Horse
62cm high and 76cm long. Unearthed from Douma Village, Xingping, Shaanxi Province. Kept in the Maoling Museum of Xingping. The harness and chariot decoration were excavated from the same pit.

and legendary palaces with bronze dragons and phoenixes flying around them.

In the Han Dynasty, there were many bronze horse sculptures. The selection and training of horses was emphasized in the Han Dynasty, and horses were considered as an important tool for the army and the state. Emperor Wudi of the Han Dynasty (reigned 140–86 BC) sent armies to Dayuan twice. Dayuan state had an abundance of strong horses. Dongmen Jing, an expert in selecting good horses, once consecrated a horse method bronze statue modeled from horses from the Dayuan state. Emperor Wudi ordered the statue be placed outside the Luban Gate of Weiyang Palace, giving an example of selecting good horses to the empire. In the early Eastern Han Dynasty, General Ma Yuan consecrated

Eastern Han. Bronze Running Horse
34.5cm high and 45cm long. Unearthed from Leitai, Wuwei county, Gansu Province in 1969.
Kept in Gansu Museum.

bronze horse statue to Emperor Guangwu (reigned 25–58), who ordered to put it in front of Xuande Palace.

These bronze horses erected on palaces have since disappeared, but a lot of bronze horses were unearthed from nobles' tombs from the Han Dynasty, such as the gilt bronze horse discovered from a nameless tomb of the Western Han in Xingping, Shaanxi, and a bronze running horse of the Eastern Han in Leitai, Wuwei, Gansu. The two bronze horses are quite delicate.

The gilt bronze horse is 62cm tall and 76cm long, in the standing pose. The neck is thin and long, legs are long and thick, and bones and muscles are well proportioned. The proportion of each part and the body structure is precise. The nose bridge is flat and the ears are like sharp bamboo. There's a cone-shaped fleshy horn on the forehead between the ears. This testifies the legend that Dayuan horses have long fleshy horns. Most bronze horses of the Han Dynasty unearthed in Fengliuling, Guixian County of Guangxi Province, Xushui of Hebei Province, and Hejiashan, Mianyang of Sichuan Province, are in running and whinnying, as if they are in the battle field.

A large group of bronze chariots and horses were discovered in a tomb of a general in late Eastern Han Dynasty, whose family name was Zhang, in Leitai, Wuwei, Gansu Province. Bronze chariots, horses and men were cast separately and then assembled and painted with colors. A bronze galloping horse, which seems unrelated to the other sculptures, is quite outstanding. The bronze sculpture is 34.5cm high. The horse is running, with one leg treading on a flying bird to maintain a stable center of gravity. The sculpture symbolizes it's a free horse running under the blue sky and white cloud and it's faster than a flying eagle. The horse's posture is elegant. Its head slightly turns to the left and its tail floats in the air. The four hooves are alternating. Although the gesture doesn't comply with the actual actions of a running horse, it maintains a dynamic balance and perfect general appearance. The five sense organs and mane are outlined with ink. The eyeballs are black, teeth white, and edges of the eyelids, mouth and nostrils are red, because a swift horse's "mouth is red and bright".

Lamps · Boshan Stove

In the Han Dynasty, noble families were abundant in their production of bronze objects for daily use, such as lamps and smoking stoves.

There are various bronze lamps, in elaborate models. Many bronze lamps were found in a tomb of the Western Han Dynasty in Mancheng, Hebei Province, including the abovementioned *Changxin* palace lamps, vermilion bird lamps, goat-cup-shaped lamps, *Danghu* lamps and three-legged lamps. In addition, lamps

Western Han. Boshan Stove with Divine Animal Pattern 26cm high and body diameter 15.5cm. Excavated from the tombs of Western Han in Mancheng, Hebei Province in 1968. Kept in Hebei Museum.

that are bull-shaped, bird-shaped with fish in bird's mouth, and links were found in Hanjiang and Suining in Jiangsu, Changsha in Hunan and Wuwei in Gansu. Some of these bronze articles can be seen as sculpture works.

Ancient people used smoking stoves to burn spices and heat the house. In the Han Dynasty, on the top of most smoking stoves were overlapping mountains. This kind of stove is called Boshan stove. After the spice was lit, smoke came out from cracks among hills, as if clouds floated over mountains, stirring people's imaginations.

Boshan stoves produced by noble families in the Han Dynasty are extremely exquisite, such as the two stoves of the Western

Han Dynasty unearthed in Mancheng, Hebei. One stove's cover has rolling hills and trees with holes, running and chasing tigers, leopards, monkeys and hunters between hills and trees. The stove stand is decorated with gilt fluffy clouds. The base features a warrior on a beast, and the warrior lifts his right hand to hold the stove's body. A gold and silver-gilt bamboo joint smoking stove was discovered in Maoling, Xingping, Shaanxi Province. According to the inscription, the stove was an imperial bronze article in Weiyang Palace. The stove is 58cm high. The round base features two deeply carved dragons, with their mouths open to hold the bamboo joint-like long handle. The bamboo joints were carved with leaves and branches. Three dragons at the end of the handle hold the stove. The upper part of the stove is in a *Boshan* shape, and the middle part is embraced by a worm. The stove bottom is decorated with 10 groups of worms on leaves. Silver and gold on the stove is closely related to the model, indicating the item was elaborately designed.

Many museums in China and overseas have collected *Boshan* stoves of the Han Dynasty in different models, which indicate the outstanding artistic talent of craftsmen at that time.

Bronze Mirrors

In terms of bronze items for daily use, the most are made up of bronze mirrors. They were used for quite a long time and there were many patterns. Most mirrors are round, some square and rectangular. The front surface is flat and is used to reflect faces, and the back

Western Han. Gilded Smoking Stove with Silver Bamboo Burl 58cm high. Unearthed from Douma village, Xingping, Shaanxi Province in 1981. Ketp in Maoling Museum. The stove has an inscription of 35 Chinese characters on the outer surface, indicating it belonged to Weiyang Palace.

Qijia Culture

Qijia Culture refers to the culture in the upper reaches of the Yellow River when the stoneware and bronze ware coexisted at the same time. It was thus named because it was first discovered in Qijiaping, Guanghe, Gansu province in 1924. Dated 2000BC to 1900 BC, it was distributed along the banks of the Yellow River and its branches in Gansu and Qinghai provinces. The residents were engaged in farming and planting millet and other plants with the bone shovels, stone knifes and stone sickles. They bred pig, sheep, dog and cattle and horse. At the time, pottery industry was well developed and copper smelting industry also made its debut.

surface has beautiful relief patterns. The button on the mirror's center was used to link it with a band. The mirror could be held with hands or placed on the wall.

The appreciation of mirror art lies in the pattern design on the back surface. The craftsman had to create an artistic layout within the limited space.

Bronze mirrors emerged during the Qijia cultural period in Gansu and Qinghai provinces, and can be found in the Shang and Western Zhou dynasties. During the Warring States Period, bronze mirror culture reached a high level in terms of the casting process and pattern design. Some mirrors are large and similar to later dressing mirrors.

Most unearthed bronze mirrors produced during the Warring States Period were discovered in Chu culture areas, such as Hunan and Anhui. Bronze mirror craftsmen were able to create various patterns that were well organized and appropriate for round shapes by using pattern composition rules. Some designs are outlined with mountain shapes, diamond and leaf shapes and decorated with dense shading, and some designs only featured feather-or cloud-shape lines. The patterns are so dense and compact that they are like silk, which were very popular at that time. Some mirrors are carved with dragons, phoenixes or other animals. The craftsmanship can be felt in every image design and combination.

Hollowing out, painting gold and silver, embedding kallaite and drawing color patterns were used to decorate bronze mirrors. A hunting-pattern, gold and silver-gild bronze mirror, which was produced during the Warring States Period, was unearthed in Jincun Village, Luoyang, Henan and transferred to Japan. The back surface is a monster growling, and the other side is an image of a knight fighting a tiger. The craftsman selected a pivotal moment of the furious fight. The knight jumps on horseback, and holds up the sword to thrust the tiger. The threatened tiger suddenly stands up on its hind legs, and growls, stretching its legs in defense. The horse is scared and steps backward. The artisan knew exactly how to capture the reactions of the knight, tiger and horse during the fight.

The Han Dynasty is the second climax of bronze mirror culture. Bronze mirrors became a necessary item in daily life and became a commodity in the Han Dynasty.

Bronze mirrors in the Western Han broke the design tradition of the Warring States Period and developed grass-leaf, star-cloud, sunlight, and Zhaoming mirrors. During the Xin Mang Period (9–23), four-immortal compass-rule mirrors were popular. The marks of T, L and V can be seen in the square frame outside the

Warring States Period. Mirror with Dragon and Phoenix Designs
Diameter 18.9cm. Excavated from tombs of the early Western Han in the south outskirts of Changsha, Hunan Province in 1954. Kept in Hunan Museum.

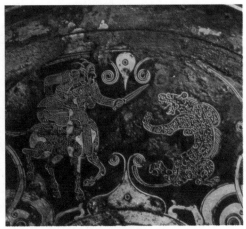

Warring States Period. Mirror Inlaid with Gold and Silver Hunting Design
Diameter 17.5cm. Unearthed from Jincun, Luoyang, Henan Province. Kept in the Eisei-Bunko Museum of Japan.
The mirror face was made of cupronickel, while the back was made of bronze.

button base. The mirror surface is equally divided. After the Xin Mang Period, the four immortals and other beast relief models became lively, and lucky character inscriptions in different types and lengths became popular. A large square bronze mirror, which weighs more than 50kg, was discovered in the tomb of Liu Xiang, the King of the Qi Kingdom during the Western Han Dynasty, in Linzi, Shandong. The mirror is 100cm long and 50cm wide. On the back of the mirror is a huge dragon design. This is the largest bronze mirror found so far in China.

After the middle of the Eastern Han Dynasty, beast and portrait mirrors in relief form were manufactured in Shanyin (today's Shaoxing, Zhejiang). These mirrors set a milestone in bronze mirror culture. Popular immortals' portraits were carved on some mirrors, and servers, winged men, musicians and lucky animals accompanied the immortals to reflect fantasy scenes. Some portraits on the mirrors are of historical figures, such as ancient emperors, Boya (a respected Qin zither master player during the

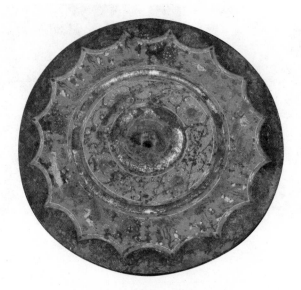

Western Han. Bronze Mirror with Chariot, Horse and Persons Painted with Color
Unearthed from Hongmiaopo, Xi'an, Shaanxi Province in 1963. Kept in Xi'an Cultural Relics
Administration of Shaanxi.

Spring and Autumn Period), and Wu Zixun (a senior official in the Wu Kingdom during the Spring and Autumn Period).

In the Han Dynasty, bronze mirror production centers spread all over the Central Plains and the northern and southern areas. The styles of the period in different places were almost identical, and the themes and representation methods were different between the Central Plains and the areas to the south of the Yangtze River.

In the late Northern and Southern Dynasties (420–589), Sui Dynasty (581–618), and Tang Dynasty (618–907), bronze mirrors that were mainly used in daily life experienced new cultural highs.

Discovering, Collecting and Studying of Bronze Ware

As the social system drastically changed after the Warring States Period, bronze ware manufacturing stopped. In the Western Han Dynasty, people couldn't identify the bronze ware names mentioned in documents that recorded the daily life and rites of the past, such as The Zhou Rituals, The Rituals, and the Book of Rites.

Imperial courts of all dynasties collected bronze ware. The discovery of ancient bronze ware was considered as a lucky case in some places and the court changed the name of the year. In the summer of 116 BC, a bronze *Ding* was unearthed in Fenshui, so the Emperor Wudi of the Han Dynasty added the character *Ding* to the name of the year. Some rulers destroyed all bronze ware collected in the courts, because they took the odd models and patterns of the bronze ware as evil symbols.

The Song and the early period of the Qing dynasties are two periods when collecting and studying bronze ware were most popular. In the 20th century, archeological excavations and systematic research were carried out on ancient bronze ware relic.

Collection and Research in the Song and Qing Dynasties

A lot of ancient bronze ware was unearthed in the Song Dynasty. The imperial court collected most of the bronze objects, and some by private collectors. In addition, quite a few manufacturers copied ancient bronze ware. This situation largely advanced the study of inscriptions or epigraphy, known as Jin Shi science. Jin means bronze ware, and Shi stands for inscriptions and portrait stones.

Scholars in the Song Dynasty recorded bronze ware collected by the imperial court and private collectors, made textual research, and identified inscriptions. The resulting research led

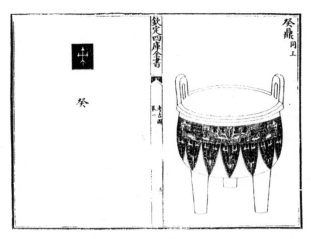

Song. Photocopy of the Archeological Drawings

to such compilations as *Archeological Drawings* by Lu Dalin, *Bogu Drawings* revised by the Emperor Huizong of the Song Dynasty, and *Continued Archeological Drawings* written by an unknown person. *Bogu Drawings* is the most important one. The book recorded 839 bronze ware articles in 20 categories.

Scholars in the Song Dynasty created the catalogue system for bronze articles. Each category of the objects in the book is accompanied by an overview, with each item copied in a three-dimensional outline, and the inscription on the article is reproduced. An explanation and textual research is provided. The size, capacity and weight of each part of the article are recorded in detail. Unfortunately, some of the copied inscriptions are distorted, and some explanations and textual research are subjective.

The number of collected bronze ware pieces in the Yuan and Ming Dynasties is small. Until the early period of the Qing Dynasty, the number of bronze ware pieces displayed in palaces and collected by the imperial court increased significantly. In the 14th year of the reign of Emperor Qianlong of the Qing Dynasty,

Emperor Qianlong ordered records of bronze ware collected by the imperial court be based on the form of *Bogu Drawings*. The records were compiled in *Xi Qing Gu Jian* in 40 volumes. The book recorded 1,529 pieces of bronze ware. Later, *Ning Shou Jian Gu* and *Xi Qing Xu Jian* were published. However, these books recorded many fake works, and had many mistakes in the various categories, naming and chronology. Researchers put too much emphasis on the textual research of inscriptions and failed to grasp the general features of bronze ware.

In the late period of the Qing Dynasty, many books concerning bronze ware research and catalogues were compiled, and quite a few were better than *Xi Qing Gu Jian* in identification and publication quality.

Bronze Ware Research in the 20th Century

In the 20th century, historians and archeologists carried out comprehensive, deep, and multi-field research on bronze ware based on scientific excavations and sufficient digging of information of bronze ware all over the country, and made remarkable academic results.

Between 1928 and 1937, the archeological group of the History and Language Research Institute of the Central Research Institute conducted 15 archeological excavations on Yinxu (Yin Ruins), capital of the late Shang Dynasty, and found the tomb of the Shang Dynasty, palace site and a great deal of carapace bone scripts and bronze ware. The excavations laid a solid foundation for the research of history, culture, and bronze ware of the Shang Dynasty. Archeological excavation on Yinxu was never interrupted. Fuhao tomb, discovered in 1976, is the tomb of a noble in the Shang imperial court. This tomb had not been discovered by anybody. The 468 bronze articles unearthed in the tomb provided precious documents for studying bronze ware types, patterns, item combinations and casting techniques during the late Shang Dynasty.

After important bronze articles in Yinxu and other places were discovered, archeological excavation reports and related theses were published. The publications are helpful for today's bronze ware research.

The Palace Museum, the National Palace Museum in Taipei, and Shanghai Museum collect a large number of ancient bronze articles. Museums in Shaanxi, Sichuan, Hunan, Hubei, Henan, Hebei, Gansu, Shanxi, Shenyang, Zhejiang, Tianjin, Yunnan, and Guangxi all have special bronze ware exhibitions. Moreover, bronze ware museums have been established in Guanghan, Guangzhou, Zhouyuan and other important excavation places.

Influential bronze ware research achievements in the first half of the 20th century consist of:

Textual Research on Bronze Ware Inscriptions of the Zhou Dynasty, written by Guo Moruo, which was published in 1932 and republished in 1958. The book recorded 137 bronze articles with specific production periods in the Western Zhou Dynasty, and 114 articles of different kingdoms in the Eastern Zhou Dynasty. The author learned from archeological methods, and carried out chronology research on bronze ware of the Western Zhou Dynasty and regional research on bronze ware of different kingdoms in the Eastern Zhou Dynasty. The research approach was innovative. The *Exploration of the Models of Yi Bronze Ware* was the opening theme of bronze ware art research.

General Research on Bronze Ware of the Shang and Zhou Dynasties, written by Rong Geng and published by Harvard-Yenching Institute in 1941, is a book that comprehensively studies Chinese bronze ware. The book has two volumes. The first volume introduces 15 bronze ware specialties, including origin, discoveries, types, epochs, inscriptions, patterns, casting processing, identification, collections, catalogues and others. The second volume collects the pictures of more than 1,000 bronze objects. Due to the limited compilation condition at that time, the identification of some items is yet to be determined. The writer cooperated with Zhang Weichi later, revised mistakes, and shortened the book to the *General Theory of Bronze Ware in the Yin and Zhou Dynasties*.

Many bronze ware research reports were published in the late period of the 20th century. Representative works include *Bronze Ware Patterns and Decorations of the Shang and Zhou Dynasty* and *Selected Bronze Ware Inscriptions of the Shang and Zhou Dynasties* compiled by the bronze ware research group of Shanghai Museum.

Spring and Autumn Period. Zengbo Qihu Kettle Shape. Inscription Rubbing

Bronze Treasures of China (16 volumes), written and edited by Li Xueqin and Ma Chengyuan, was published in 1998. The book selects 3,000 typical bronze objects from thousands of bronze items in 190 relic institutions, focusing on representative items unearthed in the second half of the 20th century, important handed down articles and items collected in countries outside of

China. The book is categorized in terms of dynasty and region. It is the most systematic collection of Chinese ancient bronze ware so far.

Bronze Ware Unearthed in Zhouyuan (10 volumes), published in 2005, organizes and studies bronze articles of the Western Zhou Dynasty and the time prior to the Zhou Dynasty in the Zhouyuan area, including Fufeng and Qishan in Shaanxi. This book's compilation structure and academic standard is higher than *Bronze Treasures of China*.

It is possible for researchers of the 20th century to obtain sufficient cultural information and directly inspect bronze articles in person, and so the understanding of bronze ware during the period is unprecedented. For example, ancient people failed to identify the purpose of a kind of vessel, so they named the vessel *Guo* or *Yi*. Modern scholar Wang Guowei and other scholars made careful studies and textual research, and drew the conclusion that the vessel is actually called *Gui*, which was used with *Ding* to contain food in ancient times. Later archeological discovery verified the deduction. Research results of historical and cultural connotations and the chronology of bronze ware inscriptions provide solid evidence for the Xia Shang Zhou Chronology Project.

Archeological discovery and research results of the 20th century also comprise of Chinese bronze ware origin research; identification of bronze ware of the Xia Dynasty, discovery and research of sacrificial pits of the ancient Shu people in Sanxingdui, Guanghan, Sichuan; discovery and research of imperial heavy bronze ware unearthed in a bronze ware hoard in Shangcheng, Zhengzhou; discovery and research of bronze ware clusters with obvious southern terrain characteristics, such as the Dayangzhou Tomb in Xingan, Jiangxi and bronze ware clusters unearthed in Jiangxi, Hunan and Hubei; continuous discovery and research of bronze ware clusters in Zhouyuan; the rules of using the *Ding* in the Western Zhou Dynasty and bronze ware chronology; research of multiculturalism in the Western Zhou Dynasty and bronze ware of kingdoms, especially the bronze ware of the Chu Kingdom after the Warring States Period, the Zenghouyi tomb unearthed in Suixian County, Hubei, and the bronze ware cluster of the king's tomb of Zhongshan Kingdom in Pingshan, Hebei; research of the bronze ware cluster of the ancient Dian people and grassland nomads; and special research of ancient bronze mirrors.

Many overseas scholars are engaged in and make contributions to Chinese bronze ware research.

Bronze ware research involves archeology, history, philology, ethnology, science and technology history, art history, and other fields. Rich relics and constant discoveries of bronze articles provide information in connection to cultural connotations, terrain features, article category names, chronology, and casting techniques. Many questions remain unanswered or unsure. Nevertheless, bronze ware research will never come to an end.

Appendix
Chronological Table of the Chinese Dynasties

The Paleolithic Period	Approx. 1,700,000–10,000 years ago
The Neolithic Age	Approx. 10,000–4,000 years ago
Xia Dynasty	2070–1600 BC
Shang Dynasty	1600–1046 BC
Western Zhou Dynasty	1046–771 BC
Spring and Autumn Period	770–476 BC
Warring States Period	475–221 BC
Qin Dynasty	221–206 BC
Western Han Dynasty	206 BC–AD 25
Eastern Han Dynasty	25–220
Three Kingdoms	220–280
Western Jin Dynasty	265–317
Eastern Jin Dynasty	317–420
Northern and Southern Dynasties	420–589
Sui Dynasty	581–618
Tang Dynasty	618–907
Five Dynasties	907–960
Northern Song Dynasty	960–1127
Southern Song Dynasty	1127–1279
Yuan Dynasty	1206–1368
Ming Dynasty	1368–1644
Qing Dynasty	1616–1911
Republic of China	1912–1949
People's Republic of China	Founded in 1949